The Board Chair
HANDBOOK

Second Edition

by Mindy R. Wertheimer

BOARDSOURCE®
Building Effective Nonprofit Boards

Library of Congress Cataloging-in-Publication Data

Wertheimer, Mindy R.

The board chair handbook / by Mindy R. Wertheimer. — 2nd ed.

     p. cm.

Prev. ed. written by William M. Dietel & Linda R. Dietel.
Includes bibliographical references.

ISBN 1-58686-094-1 (pbk.)

1. Nonprofit organizations — Management. 2. Boards of directors. I. Title.

HD62.6.D54 2007
658.4'22—dc22

2007034657

© 2008 BoardSource.
First printing, October 2007
ISBN 1-58686-094-1

Published by BoardSource
1828 L Street, NW, Suite 900
Washington, DC 20036

Building Effective Nonprofit Boards

BoardSource, formerly the National Center for Nonprofit Boards, is the premier resource for practical information, tools and best practices, training, and leadership development for board members of nonprofit organizations worldwide. Through our highly acclaimed programs and services, BoardSource enables organizations to fulfill their missions by helping build strong and effective nonprofit boards.

BoardSource provides assistance and resources to nonprofit leaders through workshops, training, and our extensive Web site, www.boardsource.org. A team of BoardSource governance consultants works directly with nonprofit leaders to design specialized solutions to meet organizations' needs and assists nongovernmental organizations around the world through partnerships and capacity building. As the world's largest, most comprehensive publisher of materials on nonprofit governance, BoardSource offers a wide selection of books, videotapes, CDs, and online tools. BoardSource also hosts the BoardSource Leadership Forum, bringing together governance experts, board members, and chief executives of nonprofit organizations from around the world.

Created out of the nonprofit sector's critical need for governance guidance and expertise, BoardSource is a 501(c)(3) nonprofit organization that has provided practical solutions to nonprofit organizations of all sizes in diverse communities. In 2001, BoardSource changed its name from the National Center for Nonprofit Boards to better reflect its mission. Today, BoardSource has approximately 11,000 members and has served more than 75,000 nonprofit leaders.

For more information, please visit our Web site, www.boardsource.org, e-mail us at mail@boardsource.org, or call us at 800-883-6262.

Have You Used These BoardSource Resources?

VIDEOS

Meeting the Challenge: An Orientation to Nonprofit Board Service
Speaking of Money: A Guide to Fundraising for Nonprofit Board Members

BOOKS

Exceptional Board Practices: The Source in Action
Managing Conflicts of Interest: A Primer for Nonprofit Boards, Second Edition
Driving Strategic Planning: A Nonprofit Executive's Guide
Taming the Troublesome Board Member
The Nonprofit Dashboard: A Tool for Tracking Progress
Presenting: Nonprofit Financials
Meet Smarter: A Guide to Better Nonprofit Board Meetings
The Nonprofit Policy Sampler, Second Edition
Getting the Best from Your Board: An Executive's Guide to a Successful Partnership
The Nonprofit Board Answer Book — A Practical Guide for Board Members and Chief Executives, Second Edition
The Source: Twelve Principles of Governance That Power Exceptional Boards
The Nonprofit Legal Landscape
Self-Assessment for Nonprofit Governing Boards
Assessment of the Chief Executive
Fearless Fundraising
The Nonprofit Board's Guide to Bylaws
Understanding Nonprofit Financial Statements
Transforming Board Structure: Strategies for Committees and Task Forces
The Board Building Cycle: Nine Steps to Finding, Recruiting, and Engaging Nonprofit Board Members, Second Edition
Culture of Inquiry: Healthy Debate in the Boardroom

THE GOVERNANCE SERIES

1. *Ten Basic Responsibilities of Nonprofit Boards*
2. *Financial Responsibilities of Nonprofit Boards*
3. *Structures and Practices of Nonprofit Boards*
4. *Fundraising Responsibilities of Nonprofit Boards*
5. *Legal Responsibilities of Nonprofit Boards*
6. *The Nonprofit Board's Role in Setting and Advancing the Mission*
7. *The Nonprofit Board's Role in Planning and Evaluation*
8. *How To Help Your Board Govern More and Manage Less*
9. *Leadership Roles in Nonprofit Governance*

For an up-to-date list of publications and information about current prices, membership, and other services, please call BoardSource at 800-883-6262 or visit our Web site at www.boardsource.org.

Contents

Introduction

As the chair of a nonprofit board of directors, you play a significant role in ensuring the organization's health and well-being. The board chair's obligation to stakeholders is to facilitate the work of the board in the context of effective leadership and good governance. The guiding principle is what's best for the organization. In this context, every board chair puts his or her own positive stamp on the board's culture, work, and impact. But many of us have served on boards where the chair's personality and personal agenda determine how the board conducts itself and what the outcomes look like. A challenge for new board chairs is to accept the power and authority of the position while putting personal interests aside in favor of the good of the organization.

In a practical sense, what does this mean for the person stepping into the board chair position? Where do you seek knowledge and guidance to help you fulfill this role? My experience with nonprofit boards as a consultant, trainer, board member, and board chair leads me to observe that there is no universal orientation or preparation. Filled with great passion and good intentions, you are expected to step into this role and know what to do. Service as a board member or committee chair does not necessarily translate into competency as a board chair. You will certainly build on what you've learned, but you'll need more than that to succeed. The unique role of the board chair requires the application of new knowledge and skills or, for others, the application of knowledge and skills in a new way.

The second edition of *The Board Chair Handbook* focuses on helping board chairs carry out their responsibilities for the good of the organization. Whether you are a seasoned board chair wanting to brush up and learn something new, an incoming board chair seeking knowledge and skills, or a person considering the possibility of becoming a board chair, this book is intended to be user friendly and practical. The guidance will also be useful to chief executives, other management personnel who interact with the board chair (including operations officers, development directors, financial officers, and marketing directors), and consultants who work with nonprofit organizations.

This book is organized into three sections:

- The Foundation: Building Individual Capacity (part I) focuses on preparing to take on the tasks and responsibilities of the board chair, beginning with an exploration of the personal decision to accept the job and covering roles, relationships, and skills.

- The Journey: Optimizing the Work of the Board (part II) deals with the application of strong leadership and sound governance practices with a focus on board process and board tasks.

- The Finale: Creating Endings and New Beginnings (part III) addresses how to prepare for the end of your term as board chair, the importance of closure, and answering, "what's next?"

Each chapter ends with a Board Chair's To Do List — brief reminders of key tasks to help you do your job effectively. Appendix 1 provides a summary of these lists. Appendix 2 provides sample agendas and letters, which are also available for free download at www.boardsource.org/bch. Throughout the book, you'll see board statistics and quotes from board members and chief executives. These data were collected during the *Nonprofit Governance Index 2007* survey, and they provide interesting insight into board service.

Readers of the first edition of *The Board Chair Handbook*, by William M. Dietel and Linda R. Dietel, published in 2001, will recognize some material in this revised edition. Special thanks to the authors for their contributions. That book, which sold more than 3,500 copies, ultimately helped thousands of organizations as their board chairs increased their understanding of their roles and responsibilities and learned techniques to make their boards more efficient and effective. Many thanks to colleagues and friends who read early drafts of my manuscript and provided helpful feedback, and to the diligent editors at BoardSource, whose contributions were invaluable in helping me find my voice in writing this book.

As you embark on the journey of leading a board, remember to build on your experiences, practice humility, follow ethical principles, and model an openness to learning that will make you the best board chair possible. When you accept the job, you enter into an obligatory relationship with the organization that is fulfilled as you adopt and model effective leadership and governance practices. Coupling these skills and practices with passion and good intentions makes a winning combination for any board chair and, ultimately, for the organization.

Part I.

The Foundation: Building Individual Capacity

To be effective as a nonprofit board chair, you need to build the individual capacity to lead and serve the organization. To begin, individual capacity building requires that you balance your personal life and your work as a board chair.

- Chapter 1 explores the many factors that you should consider when making the decision.

- Chapter 2 discusses the roles and responsibilities of the board chair position.

- Chapter 3 addresses the all-important work partnership with the organization's chief executive.

- Chapter 4 outlines the solid communications skills that the board chair's work requires — skills that invite dialogue in a nonjudgmental, respectful atmosphere.

1.

Saying Yes

The decision to serve as a board chair does not come lightly, but requires serious self-reflection. Before stepping into the position, you probably will give much thought to what this decision will mean for you, your significant others, the community, and the organization. The role of board chair is deliberate, focused, and action-oriented, and it is driven by personal passion, commitment, motivation, and leadership. The time commitment is considerable. Building individual capacity as a board chair begins with discussing the job with others, taking the time for personal reflection, evaluating your personal support system, and taking inventory of your strengths and weaknesses.

> On average, board chairs spend twice as many hours (20 vs. 10) per month on board work as do other board members.

INFORMATION GATHERING

Because the job of board chair is so critical to the organization's success, it's important to spend time finding out just what it entails. Whether you are a longtime board member or new to the organization and unfamiliar with the board, it helps to have discussions with several people inside and outside the organization:

- Ask the *current board chair* about the time commitment; challenging issues that arose during his or her tenure; unfinished board business; the strategic plan; the board's vision for the organization's direction over the next few years; and the working relationships with the chief executive, board members, community leaders, donors, and other community stakeholders.

- Ask the *chief executive* about his or her expectations of the board chair and the working relationship; vision for the organization; personal goals; and current and evolving relationships in the community. Discuss trends affecting the organization; the challenges and opportunities it faces; how it compares to similar local and national organizations; and its financial health and development plan.

- Ask the *governance committee chair* about current leadership needs; the qualities and expertise he or she thinks you bring to the board chair role; the reasons you are being considered; and the status of succession planning for other board positions.

- Ask the *treasurer* about the organization's financial health, funding sources, and funding trends. Review the annual and audit reports.

- Ask *major donors, funders, and constituents* about community perceptions and expectations of the organization; whether the quality and quantity of programs and services are fulfilling the mission; and what community issues or trends may affect the work of the organization.

These conversations will help you create a snapshot of the board chair's role as seen through the eyes of others. Such perspectives and experiences are important in acknowledging the connections between the board chair and others and creating a realistic framework for your efforts as chair. Think of this exercise as a way to begin shaping your own ideas about the work of the board chair and to identify areas warranting further exploration and possible change. As board chair, you will not necessarily follow in your predecessors' footsteps or accept what has been traditional practice. You will create a new path.

PERSONAL REFLECTION

As you consider whether to say yes, you'll need to evaluate what the decision to become board chair means to you and your significant others — including family, friends, and professional colleagues — and how this new responsibility will affect your daily life. Most of us take on a board chair role in addition to, not in place of, everything else we do in our professional and personal worlds.

A personal reflection exercise (see sidebar) will help you see yourself in the chair role, decide how you will balance the job with competing responsibilities, and evaluate your support system. Answering these questions will enable you to go forward with confidence and support and identify challenges to be addressed. Take the time to discuss your thoughts with close significant others. Being a board chair is a major commitment, but it should not consume your life. Be cognizant of achieving and maintaining a balance. You can also use this exercise if you are already a board

---

PERSONAL REFLECTION EXERCISE

- Why do I want to take on this role at this time?

- What does the organization expect from me?

- What do I expect from the organization?

- What do I expect from myself?

- What can I contribute to the organization? To the community?

- How will I balance my board chair responsibilities with my personal and professional responsibilities?

- How do my significant others feel about me taking on this role?

- How will this role affect my time with family, with friends, and at work?

- Do I have an effective support system in place?

- What do I need to do to maintain my physical and mental health as I add this role to my daily life?

chair to reassess expectations against realities, check your support system, and reflect on your self-care.

PERSONAL SUPPORT SYSTEM

Our decisions have ramifications for others in our lives, so as you consider the opportunity to become board chair, it's important to check in with those who form your personal support system. For example, you may decide that your career is on sound footing and you have reached the point in your professional life where you have more time to pursue volunteer leadership opportunities. But your spouse or partner, who has been very supportive throughout your career, may look forward to spending more time together sharing the daily routine of maintaining a household. By engaging in self-reflection coupled with discussion with significant others, you'll build a checks-and-balances system that requires reciprocal communication and shared meaning. A person may assert that one's partner is

> It's not difficult to find members, but difficult to find committed qualified members. It seems that everyone's plate is full.
>
> ~ Chief Executive

"supportive," but how does each define support, and what does support look like to each person? How are personal assumptions used in setting expectations? Have all parties come to a shared meaning? Ultimately, candid communication allows you to return to self-reflection and check your initial ideas, assumptions, and generalizations. By remaining open to feedback and discussion with others, you can uncover new information with which to alter, if necessary, your initial responses to the posed questions.

PERSONAL INVENTORY

If you are being asked to serve as board chair, you probably have at least one strength that others consider an asset or resource for the board and the organization. Through self-reflection and talking to others, you can identify your assets and areas that might benefit from improvement. Examples of strengths that enhance a board chair's capacity are

- Passion and interest

- Relationship skills

- Leadership abilities

- Subject area expertise (marketing, public relations, law, fundraising, board governance, program evaluation)

- Program area expertise aligned with the organization's purpose (arts and culture, education, health care, human services)

- Financial skills

- Community contacts

- Wealth

- Time

- Integrity

- Other strengths unique to the organization

A board chair does not need to be an expert on everything. The board is a team, and everyone brings different strengths to the table. However, a chair must have passion as well as integrity. Relationship and leadership skills can be developed over time. One incoming board chair commented that his strength is focusing on and completing tasks, but a challenge is taking the time to nurture relationships. He hoped to have a vice-chair with relationship skills to balance his focus on tasks. It's not a crime not to know; it's a crime to pretend that you do know.

BOARD CHAIR'S TO DO LIST

✓ Talk to key organizational leaders and donors to learn more about specific board chair roles and responsibilities, the current work and future direction of the organization, and others' perceptions of the organization.

✓ Think about how saying yes to serve as chair may affect your relationships at home, at work, and at leisure.

✓ Take an inventory of personal strengths and limitations, and build on this self-awareness to maximize strengths and address limited skills and knowledge areas.

2.

The Board Chair's Role

As the senior volunteer leader of the organization, the board chair is responsible for leading the board in the oversight and support responsibilities that are critical to good governance. Serving the organization's interests and needs is the foundation from which a board chair operates. A visionary board chair understands this practice and puts it into action. He or she is a generative and strategic thinker who is vigilant about asking questions and seeking knowledge to understand the opportunities, challenges, and threats that affect the organization's big picture.

Paul M. Connolly observes that visionary leaders

- attract followers and motivate people;

- focus on the big issues;

- make effectiveness a top objective;

- have the capability to set direction; and

- are willing to take calculated risks.[1]

A visionary leader empowers the board to move forward and to build organizational capacity. He or she understands that the board chair role is not about serving personal ego and preference. It is about serving the organization.

The job of board chair involves a relationship between an individual and an organization. The chair must be knowledgeable about the organization — its mission, vision, values, programs, services, constituents, and resources — and understand its place in the larger framework of the community and the still larger sphere of local and national peer organizations. With a respect for and understanding of the organization, you have a context for the board chair role. This is the foundation from which you lead. The role incorporates exhibiting leadership skills (*how* you carry out the duties) and adhering to strong governance practices (*what* duties are expected). The following list works as a board chair job description incorporating this dual focus.

> Serving on the board for my organization has been a great experience that will inspire me to become a better board member over time.
>
> ~ **Board Member**

---

1. Paul M. Connolly, *Navigating the Organizational Lifecycle: A Capacity-Building Guide for Nonprofit Leaders* (Washington, D.C.: BoardSource, 2006), p. 26.

KEY LEADERSHIP SKILLS (THE *How*)

PERSONAL QUALITIES

- Be approachable and available.

- Be a good listener and communicator.

- Show integrity, respect, and humility.

- Be a strategist, visionary, and generative thinker.

- Develop group facilitation skills.

- Encourage open communication and constructive debate.

COMMITMENT TO THE BOARD

- Engage board members to take ownership for the work of the board.

- Celebrate the hard work and achievements of individual board members and the collective board.

- Promote outstanding board development and governance practices.

COMMITMENT TO THE ORGANIZATION

- Show an understanding of and passion for the mission, values, and work of the organization.

- Engage board members to show the same commitment.

- Uphold legal and ethical standards of conduct.

KEY DUTIES (THE *What*)

CHIEF EXECUTIVE

- Cultivate a working partnership with the chief executive (see chapter 3).

- Oversee the hiring, monitoring, and evaluation of the chief executive.

BOARD MEMBERS

- Ensure that every board member carries out the roles and responsibilities of board service.

- Be the contact for board members on board issues (communication with you — not around you).

- Oversee a board assessment process.

MEETINGS

- Preside at all meetings of the board and executive committee and at other meetings or events as necessary.

- Promote meaningful dialogue at board meetings and give every board member an opportunity to contribute.

BOARD COMMITTEES

- Appoint board committee and task force chairs.

- Ensure ongoing communication with the board.

- Serve as ex officio member of all committees except the governance committee (no need to attend them all, but firsthand experience does provide insight into seeing what committee members are grappling with).

COMMUNITY

- Cultivate relationships with individual donors, funders, and other community stakeholders.

- Serve as a community ambassador and advocate for the organization.

- Speak at the annual meeting, organizational programs, and community events; and contribute to the organization's Web site, newsletter, and other communications pieces.

PARTNER WITH THE CHIEF EXECUTIVE AND BOARD MEMBERS

- Oversee fiscal affairs and organizational assets.

- Participate in strategic planning and program evaluation.

- Ensure legal and ethical compliance of all board work.

- Practice fiscal and programmatic transparency.

- Install and maintain risk management safeguards.

> Our board has come a long way, primarily because of excellent leadership from my current board chair. I believe the relationship between the chief executive and chair is absolutely critical. My current chair's strong leadership allowed this organization to take a major (and appropriate) step in reorganizing to support better legal and fiduciary relationships and to improve focus on mission.
>
> ~ Chief Executive

GETTING THE JOB DONE

It takes vigilance for a board chair to fulfill such varied responsibilities within the limits of a term of office — 1.8 years is the average term of office for a board chair with 32 percent of boards limiting the chair to two terms. A one-year term presents a challenge to adjust to the role, build the necessary relationships, and carry out the duties, and more than four years may be excessive (34 percent of boards have no limit on board chair service.) An exception might be a start-up nonprofit, in which the chair may serve for four to six years to help establish the organization and its board. At some point, however, the founding board chair needs to relinquish the position to keep the organization moving forward and to get other individuals engaged (see chapter 11 for a discussion of succession planning). Serving as board chair should never be a lifelong proposition.

TERMS OF SERVICE

52% of board chairs have terms of less than two years

33% have two-year terms

16% have terms of three or more years

Using a timetable will help you organize your time and manage the expected tasks and responsibilities. The timetable can be divided into annual, quarterly, monthly, and periodic tasks. Adding the annual meeting, board meetings, and other organizational events to the timetable will help you visualize the time commitment and its ebb and flow at various times of the year. One chief executive says that he uses the timetable, too, because it helps him stay focused on and plan for the board chair's role and tasks.

The list of tasks need not be all-inclusive because it will change as the organization responds strategically to needs and opportunities. Unexpected situations may create a shift in context and direction at any time, requiring a flexible approach by the board chair. The challenge is to move the organization forward while balancing the expected tasks with emerging exigencies and new opportunities.

SETTING A STANDARD

The board chair's role is framed by the accepted legal and ethical standards of conduct for nonprofit boards. The chair needs to stay well informed about any legal changes that will affect the functioning of the nonprofit and communicate in a clear and timely way with board members about how the changes will affect them. As the board's leader, the chair must set the example in adhering to legal and ethical standards of conduct. Ensuring compliance with these standards requires the chair to

- Apply effective communication and facilitation skills in all board discussions and deliberations

- Operate according to *what's best for the organization*

- Show transparency with full personal/professional disclosure

- Ensure that board members have all the necessary facts and figures (pro and con) when making decisions

Sample Board Chair's Timetable

Annual Tasks

Examples:

- Write speech for annual meeting
- Annual meeting
- Annual retreat
- CEO evaluation
- New board member orientation
- Contact donors for annual campaign
- Hold budget allocation meetings
- Holiday party

Weekly, Monthly, or Quarterly Tasks

Examples:

- Weekly meetings or phone calls with the chief executive
- Monthly board meetings
- Quarterly executive committee meetings
- Write newsletter column or e-mail item
- Prepare quarterly strategic planning reports

Periodic Tasks/Responsibilities

Examples:

- Fundraising events
- Committee meetings
- Advisory group meetings
- Community events
- Staff meeting presentations
- Recruitment activities
- Board education opportunities
- Board self-assessment

Most state laws governing nonprofits outline the following obligations for board members:

- Duty of care: The care that an ordinarily prudent person would exercise in a like position and under similar circumstances. A board member must exercise reasonable care — for example, stay informed, ask pertinent questions, read background materials, and participate in board deliberations — when making decisions.

- Duty of loyalty: A standard of faithfulness to the organization's welfare. A board member must show undivided allegiance — for example, avoid the prospect of personal or professional gains by disclosing potential conflicts of interest and recusing himself or herself from board discussion and voting when there is a potential conflict.

- Duty of obedience: A standard of faithfulness to the organization's mission and purpose. A board member is not permitted to act in a manner that is inconsistent with this mission, based on the public's trust to know that the organization will manage contributions in support of its mission and purpose.[2]

With the passage of the Sarbanes-Oxley Act of 2002, which requires increased fiscal oversight and transparency in publicly held corporations, nonprofit leaders have begun to address fiscal oversight and financial disclosure. Two provisions specifically require nonprofit compliance: establishing a process for employees to report alleged illegal or unethical practices in the organization without fear of punishment, and making it a crime to destroy documents to prevent their use in an official proceeding. However, Sarbanes-Oxley has triggered additional dialogue and change. Informally, nonprofit boards are responding by reexamining their transparency and accountability functions. It has been reported, for example, that most organizations with audit committees (54 percent) had created or revised the committee since 2002.[3]

In addition to maintaining legal standards of conduct, a board chair must be concerned with ethical standards of conduct, which focus on how one ought to behave. These standards include a conflict-of-interest policy. In *Managing Conflicts of Interest: Practical Guidelines for Nonprofit Boards, 2nd edition,* Daniel Kurtz and Sarah Paul point out that a board member must acknowledge the ethical obligations inherent in this role. Without adherence to ethical standards, board members may not be representing the interests of everyone the organization serves, and personal or professional interests may interfere with a board member's comportment. Evidence of ethical conduct and acting in the best interests of the organization includes

- Showing positive regard and respect for the organization and other board members

- Being trustworthy

2. Berit M. Lakey, *Nonprofit Governance: Steering Your Organization with Authority and Accountability* (Washington, D.C.: BoardSource, 2000), p. 25.

3. Francie Ostrower and Marla J. Bobowick, "Nonprofit Governance and the Sarbanes-Oxley Act," Urban Institute National Survey of Nonprofit Governance: Preliminary Findings, 2006. p. 2; http://www.urban.org/UploadedPDF/311363_nonprofit_governance.pdf

WHEN BOARD MEMBERS ARE APPOINTED

Sometimes a board member is appointed by virtue of his or her affiliation with another organization and represents that organization on the board. One board had appointees mandated by the state, creating the unintentional side effects of competing self-interests and minimal focus on what was in the best interests of the organization. However, most states legislate nonprofit standards of conduct, and so board members who are appointed as "organizational representatives" need to be versed in the legal and ethical obligations of board service. The board chair could help educate representative organizations on these obligations so that future appointees will have a better sense of the expectations of board membership. It might be necessary to outline the standards of conduct and have them placed prominently in the boardroom. Every board, whether it has appointed or elected members, has the right to full stewardship from its members.

- Exercising authority as appropriate

- Displaying courteous conduct

- Maintaining confidentiality

- Speaking with one voice upon stepping out of the boardroom

- Disclosing information to assess possible board member conflicts

The board chair needs to model these behaviors, encourage them in fellow board members, and intervene when unethical conduct is displayed. If there is a conflict of interest, the chair may have to ask a board member to recuse himself or herself from a discussion or activity.

One board holds a formal orientation for new board members where the board chair addresses the legal and ethical standards of conduct. Each new board member is given a form to read and sign acknowledging his or her understanding of and abidance to the legal and ethical standards of conduct governing the role as a board member.

BOARD CHAIR'S TO DO LIST

✓ Be a visionary leader. Empower the board to be innovative, creative, and take calculated risks.

✓ Develop and apply key leadership skills (including respect, humility, integrity, and communication) in accomplishing the key duties of the board chair role.

✓ Decide how you will balance routine tasks and those that surface unexpectedly.

✓ Uphold ethical and legal standards of conduct, and expect no less from every board member.

3.

The Board Chair-Chief Executive Partnership

The board chair's relationship with the chief executive is by far the most important relationship he or she will have. It is critical to forge a working partnership that begins even before you officially become board chair. When you are considering the position, begin an informal dialogue with the chief executive as part of your personal reflection on the possibilities and challenges.

In combining resources, a partnership's whole becomes greater than its individual parts. The partnership between the board chair and the chief executive has the capacity to transform an organization and move it forward. It is the face of the organization. One board chair and chief executive co-presented a new program request to a funding organization. The funder was quite impressed with their teaming. Their strong partnership was viewed as representing a strong organization. As board chair, you need to understand this partnership, help make it work, and use it to the advantage of the organization.

> Our board is great and has enabled us to grow and expand to meet the needs of the community. Board members are supportive of staff and understand the differences between their responsibilities and those of management.
>
> ~ Chief Executive

Like any relationship, the board chair-chief executive partnership requires commitment and effort from both partners. Each should take responsibility for his or her behaviors and actions and be open to constructive feedback not just on the tasks at hand, but on the partnership itself. Three basic principles are the foundation of a strong partnership:

- Mutual respect, trust, and support for each other and the partnership

- Reciprocal communications

- Shared purpose

With these principles in place, the board chair and chief executive should be equipped to understand one another's perspectives as they build the leadership partnership. Their goals will include

- Adapting to differences in personality, temperament, work style, communication style, and time commitment

- Keeping ongoing tasks and responsibilities running smoothly during board leadership transitions

- Setting mutual expectations for the working relationship

- Establishing clear boundaries for roles and responsibilities and understanding where they overlap

- Agreeing on what sound governance practices are and how to apply them

- Developing a shared interpretation of what constitutes the best interests of the organization

The two leaders will not always agree on the issues they face (and that is not necessarily the objective), but each voice should be heard and respected while framed by a shared purpose. The chief executive may already have expectations for how his or her relationship with the board chair operates based on past experience and personal preference. These expectations may be different from how you perceive the working relationship. As board chair, you need to take the initiative to articulate your view of the working relationship and go over the three guiding principles.

HIERARCHY VS. PARTNERSHIP

It is important to understand when to make joint decisions and when to exert authority. The chief executive works at the pleasure of the board, possibly creating an imbalance in the chair-executive partnership. Tension may be discernible when the executive's contract is up for renewal or when it is time for an annual salary review. As board chair, you should engage a compensation committee (including counsel) to negotiate the contract and recommend a salary increase based on preset variables stated in the executive's contract, such as the performance evaluation and annual goals. When there is this sense of imbalance in the partnership, do not back away from applying the partnership principles — consciously use them.

DEFINING SEPARATE AND SHARED RESPONSIBILITIES

In some cases, tensions between the chair and chief executive stem from confusion over who is responsible for what. Even board members and staff may have trouble distinguishing between the two leaders' responsibilities. Be clear about job responsibilities from a solid governance perspective, not based on individual preferences. The board chair role is outlined in chapter 2 and may be outlined in your organization's bylaws or board manual. To understand the chief executive's role, ask to see the job description (a board chair should receive a copy of this document). How does the chief executive see his or her role in relation to the job description? How does the board chair see it? Sit down and discuss mutual expectations and definitions around the traditional management-governance distinctions, and identify tasks (such as fundraising, strategic planning, and succession planning) that benefit from shared responsibility. Have this discussion in the context of the organization's strategic goals, which are the basis for identifying annual tasks. *The Ten Basic Responsibilities of Nonprofit Boards*, by Richard T. Ingram, and *The Nonprofit Chief Executive's Ten Basic Responsibilities*, by Richard L. Moyers, may be helpful to you in this process.

One example related to defining responsibility is who creates the board meeting agenda. It may seem expedient for the chief executive to develop the agenda, but this practice may give the appearance that he or she is dictating or manipulating the work of the board. Reality or not, this perception is the antithesis of what the board chair strives to achieve. To conduct the work of the board, the board chair needs to have input into this process. Both perspectives are needed in creating the agenda. The chief executive brings agency operations and updates, industry trends, and community issues for consideration. The board chair brings a more detached view of the big picture with focus on governance responsibilities. Creating the board meeting agenda should be a shared task, but the board chair has ultimate responsibility for what is to be covered at the meeting.

> I think it is difficult sometimes for board members to see the demands on the chief executive. They tend to see only their request or interest, and it is difficult to share the whole picture with them without appearing to be whining or complaining about the workload.
>
> ~ Chief Executive

COMMUNICATION

Supporting the chief executive is one way the board chair can also support the organization. Open communication on a weekly basis is highly important, whether by e-mail, telephone, video conferencing, in person, or some combination. You may discuss a specific item or simply check in to see how things are going. You should have at least one in-person meeting each month over breakfast, lunch, or coffee, inside or outside the office, but in a quiet space where confidentiality can be maintained. In national organizations where the board chair and chief executive live in different places, meetings may be a challenge, so you should make an extra effort to use other forms of communication.

Make it clear to the chief executive from the start that the board wants to keep abreast of problems as they occur, along with trends, opportunities, or general concerns that are worthy of discussion. No board chair likes surprises. You will want transparency and accountability in all transactions and interactions and, therefore, frequent communication is essential. Similarly, you owe it to the chief executive to keep him or her informed of any board concerns about the effective operations of the board and the organization. It is your responsibility to ensure that board members who may have direct contact with the chief executive, such as the treasurer or other committee chairs, bring any concerns about their relationships with the executive to you instead of voicing them directly. If it seems that the chief executive is under constant bombardment by board members, then it is the chair's responsibility to act as a gatekeeper, and determine a more concise flow of information.

If communication difficulties with the chief executive escalate to the point where only the intervention of an objective third party can help, it could be useful to ask a consultant to mediate and help arrive at a solution. If the conflict relates to a governance issue, a board governance consultant may be helpful.

PROFESSIONAL BOUNDARIES

The board chair and chief executive must have a professional relationship with clear boundaries. However, as the partnership develops, you may share personal information as you get to know one another, adding a humanizing element and creating a less perfunctory relationship. You may also gain a larger context of understanding about what each of you brings to your role.

It's important to be aware of how the personal may affect the professional. For example, if either the chief executive or board chair faces an emergency with a family member, how will the other person's responsibilities be handled? How can you help each other, and, if necessary, how can another staff or board member temporarily step up to assist the organization? Avoid allowing the personal relationship to dominate the professional one.

TIPS FOR A POSITIVE RELATIONSHIP

1. Communicate openly and often, sharing both good and bad news.

2. Address concerns and sensitive issues.

3. Keep individual egos in check, and don't compete for the limelight.

4. Be considerate and respectful.

5. Clarify and share mutual expectations about roles and responsibilities in the context of a shared purpose.

6. Work within the limits placed on the relationship, such as those established in agency bylaws and policies or by a national association or accrediting body.

7. Acknowledge each other's contributions to the work of the partnership.

PARTNERSHIP CHALLENGES

How the board chair and chief executive resolve the challenges in their relationship sets the tone for the board chair's term in office and may affect other board and staff relationships, creating additional tensions, divided loyalties, and unwelcome schisms.[4] If the differences are unchecked, the work of the board suffers.

---

4. *The Nonprofit Board Answer Book: A Practical Guide for Board Members and Chief Executives*, 2nd ed. (Washington, D.C.: BoardSource, 2007).

Part of the challenge in forging a partnership is dealing with uncomfortable issues and problems. Often, new board chairs are not quite sure how to use their authority. At times this uncertainty looks like compliance with the norm. For example, one incoming board chair remarked that her chief executive routinely chooses the members of the nominating committee and was a member himself. She was content to follow the current organizational practices and assumed it was acceptable. By simply accepting a "routine" practice without assessing it from the perspective of good governance practices, this board chair let personal issues take precedence over good governance. Challenging a strong chief executive is not an easy task for a new board chair (or even an existing one), but in the context of good governance and effective leadership, challenging old practices may need to occur.

Both you and the chief executive bring your personal histories to the partnership, creating interactions different from each past one. Outside variables may enter into the equation to complicate the board chair-chief executive partnership:

- Gender similarities or differences

- Age similarities or differences

- Ethnic, cultural, or religious similarities or differences

- Tenure of the chief executive (new or veteran)

- Work and volunteer history, occupation of the board chair

- Personality type (quiet or overbearing)

- Range of communication skills

- Assertiveness or lack thereof

- Degree of confidence in oneself and in the other person

- Personal integrity or lack thereof

- Fear of hurting one another's feelings, making waves, opening Pandora's box, undermining current practices

- Feeling overwhelmed or being in over one's head

- Feeling uncertain, intimidated, unmotivated, anxious

Consciously or unconsciously, these variables can easily undermine the working relationship and the balance of power between the chair and the chief executive. Building a collaborative relationship requires finding common ground from which to operate while respecting your differences. Your attention to the partnership must focus on the reality and the perception. For example, one chair expressed reservations about the chief executive's role in financial matters. The chief executive appeared to maintain control over budget issues and would not share information as requested with the board chair or treasurer. Asserting herself, the current board chair initiated a discussion with the chief executive on role expectations. The chair had to put aside her own issues, such as having less financial experience, avoiding confrontation, and fearing stepping on the executive's turf, to focus on her board leadership role.

SUPERVISING THE CHIEF EXECUTIVE — THE BOARD CHAIR'S ROLE

Representing the board, the board chair is the chief executive's primary supervisor. Every board member cannot serve this function. Imagine a workplace where you were accountable to five to 40 *direct* supervisors! Board members will have direct contact with the chief executive in working on projects and tasks, but if there are problems in these relationships, the board chair needs to be informed. At the same time, the chief executive may have problems with a board member and this, too, should be discussed with the board chair. The chief executive and board members must know the process for dealing with concerns in these relationships. Even though the board chair is the conduit between the chief executive and the board, all board members should give their feedback in the executive's annual performance evaluation.

BOARD CHAIR'S TO DO LIST

✓ Frame the partnership in the context of good governance practices.

✓ Be sensitive to the many variables that can influence the success or failure of this key relationship, and have the courage to act to bring about change.

✓ Have clear mutual expectations around roles and responsibilities.

✓ Maintain open lines of communication.

✓ Periodically assess the health of the partnership in the areas of trust, respect, communication, purpose, expectations, attitudes, and boundaries.

4.

Communication and Facilitation Skills

Strong communication skills are essential to the role of the board chair, who will need to facilitate board meetings and represent the organization in different settings and situations. Some circumstances — such as board meetings — require the chair to create an atmosphere in which everyone is invited to share their opinions through facilitated discussion and dialogue. In other contexts — such as meetings with funders — you will represent the organization and communicate on its behalf. We often assume that anyone who becomes a board chair already is a good communicator, but that is not necessarily the case. The following basic skills and pointers will help make you a stronger communicator.

INDIVIDUAL COMMUNICATION SKILLS

LISTENING

The board chair should be the role model for an effective listener. Listening takes energy, focus, and patience. You may hear some of the facts and details but miss the real meaning or complete message, especially when you have something else on your mind or are distracted by other conversations. A focused listener can

- ask a question for more clarification;

- make a statement to provide clarification or information;

- respond with empathy to show understanding;

- use confrontation to identify a discrepancy, distortion, or contradiction; and

- make an appropriate transition to another topic.

It is important to strike a balance between listening to what the other person has to say and then responding in context, and having a preplanned agenda for what you need to say without regard for other comments.

As board chair, you may need to break bad listening habits that have developed over time. It helps to take a personal inventory using the Listening Skills Exercise (see sidebar). Ask for feedback from others to help you address the needed changes.

LISTENING SKILLS EXERCISE

Identify strengths:

1. How does my nonverbal behavior show that I am listening?

2. How do my verbal responses show that I am listening?

3. How do I put the speaker at ease?

4. How do I show interest in and respect for the speaker?

5. What are my strengths as a listener?

Identify listening habits:

1. Do I pretend to listen, but my nonverbal communication gives me away?

2. Do I pretend to listen, but I am bored, distracted, or daydreaming?

3. Do I hear the facts but miss the real meaning of the message?

4. Am I preoccupied with my own agenda, which prevents me from listening?

5. Do I interrupt others?

6. Do I have selective listening?

7. Do I make assumptions about the message without listening fully to what is actually being said?

8. Do I respond defensively?

9. Am I reactive or impatient?

10. Do I multitask while I am listening?

During board meetings, remember these two basic principles of listening:

1. Don't simply ignore what a person has to say, even if it is off topic. Show respect by conveying that you heard the comment. For example, "I appreciate your concern for the ABC program, which we can address at another time, but today we need to discuss the community outreach project." Or, "You seem to have some strong concerns about the fundraising event, but as a board, we had agreed to move forward with it. Since we have other agenda items and limited time, let's see if we can find some other time to talk about it."

2. Don't pretend to listen. Stay focused on board members' remarks. When distracted, ask the other board members: "Who can help summarize this discussion?" The chair can offer a summary as well and then ask the board to help fill in what has been missed.

Using Questions

Questions encourage the communication of relevant information. When used appropriately, questions offer some direction without restricting the response or being suggestive. In forming questions, choose between closed- and open-ended questions. Closed-ended questions begin with do, does, did, have, is, should, could, or would. They invite a simple yes-no or one-word response. Open-ended questions seek a more open, detailed response and usually begin with what or how. Ask yourself what is the intent of your question and what type of response you are seeking. Some examples:

Closed-ended	Open-ended
Do you want the committee chair to present to the board?	*What* are your thoughts about having the committee chair present to the board?
Do you think it is a mistake to do this fundraiser?	*What* are the risks of doing this fundraiser?
Should I recommend the program changes at the next meeting?	*How* should I present the recommended program changes to the board?
Is she attending the task force meetings?	*How* is she contributing to the task force deliberations?

Framing the appropriate question takes some thought. A board chair has the responsibility to ensure clarity and not lead a person's response in one direction or another. Remember these pointers:

1. Don't ask leading or suggestive questions that put words in the other person's mouth and show no respect for his or her opinion: "You *do* want to build that new facility, *don't you?*" "What do you think of Jane's *ridiculous* idea?" "Do you *really* want to handle it that way?"

2. Don't ask double questions. When a person is eager to gather information, two or more questions may be asked at the same time. The response will usually be to the second of the two questions, and the first question is lost.

Probing for Shared Meaning

"He is doing great as treasurer." "I think our board meeting went well." "The board member seemed agitated." Without additional probing to uncover the meaning of the words in each of these comments, you might assume that you have achieved shared meaning, but in fact the meaning is incomplete. The treasurer is great because he shows up for meetings? Initiated a new accounting system? Is personable? Explains the budget in terms that everyone understands? The board meeting went well because it was quick? No one argued? There was debate? Sue wasn't there? The materials were helpful? A decision was made? The board member was agitated because she had a bad day at work? Didn't like what Jim said about the strategic plan? Didn't like coming out in the rain tonight? Got a speeding ticket today?

What do great, well, and agitated mean in these examples? You need to ask rather than assume: "Give me an example of what you mean by 'great'." "What do you mean by it 'went well'?" "What do you mean by 'agitated'?" Establishing shared meaning requires probing for further details and not accepting words and statements at face value. Do not assume that you understand what is said. We sometimes create meaning that differs from what the speaker intended. If you do not probe for clarification, you cannot achieve shared meaning, and consequently, decisions may be made based on assumptions, inaccurate or limited information, and false meaning.

EMPATHY

When you show empathy, you understand a person's message, provide support, and encourage dialogue and clarity. Empathy supports all voices being heard and understood in the process of deliberating, creating consensus, and completing tasks.

An astute board chair can listen to a person's verbal message and, at the same time, understand the feeling behind the message and communicate it back to the speaker. The key to expressing empathy is thinking *with* the person, not for or about him or her. It means going beyond the nonempathic response of "I understand what you mean."

> **Board member:** "This donor refuses to acknowledge our organization's need to engage in community outreach."
> **Board chair:** "You seem somewhat frustrated by the donor's response to our community outreach plan."

> **Committee chair:** "We had productive discussions and completed a list of recommendations with just three meetings!"
> **Board chair:** "It sounds like you are extremely pleased with the work of your committee."

> **Board member:** "I appreciate the opportunity for open, candid board discussions and want to continue contributing to the dialogue."
> **Board chair:** "It sounds like being an active, engaged board member is important to you."

> **Treasurer:** "I have been treasurer for two other nonprofits during the past six years."
> **Board chair:** "You certainly bring a wealth of knowledge to this position, and I hope you can share some of it to help educate our board about fiscal affairs."

> **Chief executive:** "Meeting with the board chair twice a month has always worked well for me in the past."
>
> **Board chair:** "It sounds like you want to continue this arrangement and would feel a bit hesitant to make a change."

When expressing empathy, do so with flexibility and tentativeness rather than stating a fact. Frame the statement with *perhaps, it sounds like, it appears,* or *it seems.* This approach allows the other person to let you know whether you have hit the mark and truly understand the original message.

CONFRONTATION AND ASSERTIVENESS

Confrontation is a difficult communication skill to apply appropriately. It requires taking responsibility for what you say and presenting the message in an assertive manner without putting the respondent on the defensive. Confrontation is used when there are

- differing perceptions of a situation or circumstance;

- contradictory comments, attitudes, and behaviors being expressed verbally or nonverbally; or

- issues or concerns being ignored or not raised.

These conditions interfere with achieving responsible, frank, and constructive discussions, and ultimately they may hinder the quality of the discussion outcomes. Using confrontation requires an assertive response, which means taking responsibility by using "I" messages. Such messages require a tentative rather than an accusatory tone to give the respondent room to respond. The goal is to enhance communication, not force the respondent to shut down.

> **Board chair:** "You say that you support this resolution, but I get the sense that you have some genuine concerns. What are your thoughts?"
>
> **Board chair:** "So far we have only heard the pros of this fundraising opportunity. What are the down sides to it?"
>
> **Board chair:** "I have a different take on it. I am wondering if it was not a malicious response at all, but rather one reflecting limited facts and information."
>
> **Board chair:** "Part of board membership requires your presence at board meetings. I am concerned that you have not attended the last three meetings."

Group Facilitation Skills

One-on-one communication skills — listening, question formulation, probing for shared meaning, empathy, and confrontation — become the foundation for group facilitation skills. For a board chair, the challenge is to apply these skills in dialogue with a group of individuals. As a group facilitator, you must show attentiveness, responsiveness, and flexibility toward the group process and, at the same time, acknowledge and respond to individual comments — all while respecting the allotted time and focusing on the task at hand. It requires skill to direct participants' comments to remain on task and to help clarify and summarize points that others are making. The objective is to facilitate candid discussions of complex issues or the task at hand without "unwittingly encouraging board members to suppress or channel dissent in destructive ways." Dissent does not equal disloyalty, but rather is a sign that inquiry and robust discourse are valued.[5]

As group facilitator, you should check with other board members for their reactions and thoughts about needed clarification and suggestions or comments made by others. Encourage everyone's participation. Support the following group process ground rules:

- Everyone has a voice.

- Everyone has a right to be heard.

- Be respectful and considerate of others.

- Only one person speaks at a time, and no one person dominates the dialogue.

At times, a board chair may need to challenge board members who do not appear to be listening or engaged — sending e-mails on their hand-held computers, conducting side conversations, or simply daydreaming. You may also need to challenge board members who are overly engaged — perhaps interrupting, making aggressive comments that attack or judge others, or dominating discussions. Both behaviors are inappropriate, and they require action by the board chair to reinforce the ground rules and hold each member accountable. The board chair must provide the leadership to manage the board process, which includes responding to troublesome behaviors by a board member, as reinforced in Katha Kissman's *Taming the Troublesome Board Member*. Egregious behavior may best be addressed outside the boardroom in a meeting with the board member to discuss, by sharing specific examples, how his or her behavior is disruptive to the work of the board.

Working within the time constraints of a board meeting requires skill as a group facilitator and realism when creating a meeting agenda. Don't be overly ambitious with a long agenda, which may push you to facilitate on a "fast forward" mode and limit the board's effectiveness. If you need a quick decision and members are still deliberating, you may ask to remove the next agenda item, if appropriate. Or you may facilitate closure of the discussion and help the board decide what should happen next: allow further board discussion now, send the matter back to the committee or task force, or move for a vote or final decision.

---

5. Nancy Axelrod, "Curious Boards," *Board Member*, May/June 2006, p. 9.

You may need to be creative in giving each board member a voice within the prescribed timeframe of a meeting. One board chair divided her large board into smaller groups for purposeful discussion. She formed board member dyads and asked each dyad to generate a list of ideas for volunteer recruitment. Three dyads then formed small groups, and each group generated a list culled from the contributions of each dyad. The full board came together for discussion and developed a final list based on the work of the small groups. Ultimately, every board member contributed to the final product.

BOARD CHAIR'S TO DO LIST

✓ Focus on both the intent and delivery of the message being communicated.

✓ Apply communication skills differentially, taking into account the purpose of the exchange and the audience.

✓ Strengthen communication skills by listening, formulating proper questions, probing to achieve clarification and shared meaning, demonstrating empathy, confronting difficult issues or obstacles, and being attentive to content and group dynamics.

✓ Practice and ask for feedback from others on your use of effective communication and facilitation skills.

Part II

The Journey: Optimizing the Work of the Board

The board chair's leadership responsibilities and governance duties to optimize the work of the board fall into two broad categories: board process and board tasks. Board process is about building a strong team, and board tasks are what the team needs to accomplish. The board chair must sustain this dual focus to create a high-performing board that adds value to the organization. If you understand board process and work to enhance your knowledge and skills in that area, you will optimize the outcomes of board tasks. This section addresses both process and tasks, with an emphasis on process.

- Chapter 5 deals with the board development model that emphasizes the importance of cultivating board relationships. This model is the foundation for board process.

- Chapter 6 explores successful decision making, a critical factor, and explains the necessity of all viewpoints, ideas, facts, opinions, and questions being placed on the table as part of generative thinking.

- Chapter 7 discusses the need for understanding and application of different work structures to frame the work of the board and enhance communications.

- Chapter 8 deals with resource development and fiscal oversight.

- Chapter 9 explains the board chair's role in strategic and program planning.

- Chapter 10 details the benefits of performance evaluation for the board and the chief executive.

5.

Board Development

Effective board development practices help each board member develop a sense of ownership, responsibility, and commitment to the mission, vision, and values of the organization. If a board is functioning at its optimal level, chances are the organization is as well. Vibrant, healthy, responsive, forward-thinking boards tend to support vibrant, healthy, responsive, forward-thinking organizations. Board development provides a structure to maximize each board member's contributions to the board and the organization. Each individual should have a voice, feel valued, and play a compelling role as a team member.

> We spend a great deal of time vetting out the "right fit" for the culture of the board. We understand that personality plays an important role in the board dynamic. We have several rounds of meetings with each potential candidate.
>
> ~ Chief Executive

Developing, educating, or building a board all have the same objective: to create an effective board that is conscious of its own role and responsibilities, motivated by the mission of the organization, willing and able to participate actively in board leadership, and qualified to guide the organization forward. The board chair is responsible for ensuring that comprehensive board development initiatives are in place. A governance committee, in partnership with the board chair and the chief executive, leads these initiatives.

A typical board development model has three purposes: to identify and engage individuals as potential board members; to maximize each board member's contributions to the board; and to maintain engagement of outgoing board members. Board development activities can be organized in four categories, each with a distinct target audience:

> We aim high. These people are very busy; we need to get in their pipeline for board service. We also do not compromise on our requirements for board service.
>
> ~ Chief Executive

- Identification (potential board members)

- Orientation (new board members)

- Sustainability (ongoing board members)

- Preservation (outgoing board members)

IDENTIFICATION

The foundation of board development is identifying potential board members and creating opportunities for engagement and leadership development. Identification begins with each contact a board or staff member has in the community with volunteers, organizational members, other service providers, consumers, or clients.

Each contact may be an opportunity to identify a potential board candidate. One never knows who will ultimately become the next board member. Identifying future board members is a shared task between the board and senior staff. The board chair appoints a governance committee to lead the process, considering both short-term and long-term board needs.

Most board members were recruited by another board member (54%), by the organization's chief executive (37%) or by members of the organization (15%). Few (9%) sought out a board seat on their own, and fewer still came to a board through a corporate board placement program (1%) or board matching program (1%).

Boards have different ways of assessing candidate interest and potential. One organization invites prospective members to attend leadership training sessions where they can learn more about the organization. These sessions are good indicators of whether serving on the board or as a volunteer in another capacity would be a good fit. From the prospective member's perspective, this preliminary training shows the organization's commitment to leadership development. (See sample recruitment letter in Appendix 2.)

As board chair, you have these responsibilities in board member identification:

- Network in the community to identify new volunteers and lay leaders. Initiate discussion about the organization and assess interest or curiosity. Make sure that someone from the organization follows through in contacting any leads.

- Attend organizational events geared to increasing individual engagement. Speak passionately about your work on behalf of the organization as well as the organization's contributions to the community.

- Participate in leadership-building or mentoring programs. Show that the board is welcoming and committed to building new leaders.

- Be visible.

ORIENTATION

For new board members, board orientation helps to

- develop an understanding of the organization;

- develop an understanding of board member roles and responsibilities;

- increase confidence and comfort level with board service; and

- cultivate relationships with current board members.

New members joining the board should have some familiarity with the organization's mission, goals, vision, finances, programs and services, and other basic details before their first board meeting. They should also have information about the functions of the board and their role as board members. Most new board members find a board orientation program to be the best way to learn what they need to know. The board chair works closely with the chief executive and the governance committee to plan and present this program.

Orientation features presentations by the board chair, the chief executive, select board members, and other senior staff members. The board chair and board members explain what is expected in terms of attendance, behavior, standards of conduct, confidentiality, board responsibilities, conflict of interest, financial contributions, and relationships with the staff. The chief executive and staff cover the organization's history, current programs, purpose, strategic plan, and other pertinent information. New board members should receive a comprehensive board manual that includes much of this information and can be used as a reference. Additional organizational information should include

- Bylaws and policies

- Strategic plan

- Organizational chart

- Board member list and contact information

- Board structure and committees

- Annual report and Form 990

Between the orientation and the board manual, new board members should have a good foundation for attending and participating in their first board meeting.

After the orientation or before the first board meeting, many organizations host a social hour for new board members to meet their colleagues. Consider inviting past board chairs to represent the rich continuum of the organization's board leadership. A mentoring program is a good tool for new board members, and it supports the effectiveness of both incoming and seasoned members. A mentor-mentee relationship is a safe haven where a new member can air questions and concerns that he or she may hesitate to raise elsewhere.

Beyond your presentation at the orientation program, you have other responsibilities as board chair:

- Make sure each new board member meets with the chair and the chief executive. These informal sessions are a reciprocal opportunity to get to know one other, to begin identifying the new member's strengths and interests, and to answer questions about the board and the organization. If board members are required to serve on a committee or task force, they can use this meeting to explore options. In some organizations, the meetings are held with both the chair and the chief executive present.

- Delegate a board member or committee to oversee mentoring of new board members.

- As appropriate, schedule meetings with the chief executive and each new board officer or member who has a portfolio responsibility (for example, resource development, program planning and evaluation, strategic planning).

- Be engaged.

SUSTAINABILITY

Sustaining the interest, engagements, and abilities of board members serves to

- enhance their sense of ownership, responsibility, leadership, and accountability as organizational stewards;

- strengthen their working relationships with one another; and

- sustain quality governance and decision making.

As board chair, you need to cultivate strong one-on-one relationships with each board member. Show respect for and value each person, engage in open communication, be empathic and nonjudgmental, create trustworthiness, and do not ignore or take for granted anyone's contributions.

For the board chair, building and sustaining relationships is an ongoing process that helps you engage and be engaged — not a one-time activity with new board members. The board chair's relationships with experienced board members keep you connected to their changing and developing interests. It is easy to assume that an individual will simply continue serving in the same capacity year after year: same committee assignment, same task force, or same focus in an area of expertise. One board chair wrapped up her first year in office by making personal contacts with every member to ask about his or her committee work. Board service is more satisfying when a person has the chance to change assignments and explore new interests.

> One of our board's biggest challenges is how to actively engage board members between meetings. Board membership entails more than coming to meetings.
>
> ~ Chief Executive

The board chair should identify opportunities for board members to build individual leadership capacity, which serves a dual purpose: getting work done and planning for board leadership succession. By asking board members to serve as mentors for new board members and to lead initiatives or tasks outside their areas of expertise or comfort zone, you will cultivate relationships and nurture leadership potential in people who can function from multiple perspectives, not just from what they know or do best.

In addition to relationship building, promoting board sustainability includes these responsibilities for a board chair:

- Focus on board communications (see chapter 7), including

  - Work with the chief executive to ensure that members receive useful meeting materials in enough time to review them.

  - Use group facilitation skills and other creative techniques to enhance discussion, communication, and decision making at board meetings.

  - Speak at training sessions for committee and task force chairs about their role supporting the work of the board and the formal board reporting process.

- Work with the chief executive to determine which reports should be presented to the board.

- Hold periodic board retreats. The focus depends on the board's needs related to process and tasks as well as big-picture issues.

- Schedule comprehensive board self-assessments, which includes board feedback and action items. Self-assessment is a sign that the board takes its work seriously, is open to constructive feedback, and acknowledges that there is always room for improvement (see chapter 10).

- Delegate leadership responsibilities to board members.

- Encourage other board members to attend community and organizational events.

- Be available.

PRESERVATION

Preserving relationships with former board members and board chairs, an important focus of board development, benefits the organization because these leaders will

- feel gratified that they have made a contribution;

- continue in their roles as organizational ambassadors; and

- find new opportunities for engagement.

Remembering that so much time and effort have been invested in building strong and significant relationships for the good of the organization, why stop when an individual's board term has expired? In fact, most board members stay involved with their organization after leaving the board.

Though the momentum to preserve these relationships must continue, the shift in roles must be clearly understood. Sometimes board members may find it difficult to relinquish the power and authority of the board role. Instead, they can take on new volunteer responsibilities. One organization asked an outgoing board chair to lead a task force of former board chairs to plan an anniversary celebration.

As board chair, you can preserve relationships with outgoing board members in a number of ways:

- Convey your personal thanks. You might host a social event, make a phone call, write a note, make a donation to the organization in honor of the board member, or publicly acknowledge him or her at a board or annual meeting.

- Provide the opportunity for closure and show respect for their contributions. Consider setting aside time at the final board meeting for each person who wants to speak, or delegate a committee or task force to conduct exit interviews.

- Attend recognition events to honor past board members and board chairs.

- Identify and individualize opportunities for ongoing involvement, such as task forces, strategic planning, and special projects.

- Be gracious.

BOARD DEVELOPMENT CHALLENGES

The board chair, chief executive, and governance committee invest considerable time and effort in creating and implementing a comprehensive board development plan. Ultimately, each of the four categories in the model — identification, orientation, sustainability, and preservation — is about building relationships. As board chair, you will concentrate primarily on sustainability to optimize the current work of the board. Here are some of the more delicate challenges you may face:

A DIVIDED BOARD

Effective boards include individuals with diverse talents, expertise, backgrounds, and points of view. Differences of opinion are a sign of a vibrant, healthy board. But when differences escalate into divisions, they can prevent the board from making good decisions. As board chair, you are responsible for resolving conflicts. If you cannot handle a situation as an objective mediator, you

> Board policy, procedures, and strategies must be in place before recruiting board members, and those members should be strategically selected. There is a great difference between sitting on a board and serving on a board.
>
> ~ Chief Executive

may need to ask the vice-chair, another board member, or even a consultant to step in. It may be appropriate to delegate responsibility for conflict resolution to the executive committee or a special task force.

A DOMINEERING OR INTIMIDATED BOARD MEMBER

The task of running a board meeting involves giving everyone a chance to contribute while not allowing one or a few members to dominate the discussion or intimidate others. A board may have a few members who seem to make all the decisions while the rest of the board acts as a rubber stamp. You should be aware of group dynamics and apply facilitation skills, making sure that more members have a voice by limiting each person's time to talk if necessary and drawing out comments from quieter members. You may need to talk privately with a member who frequently speaks out of turn, dominates discussions, or is verbally aggressive. These behaviors may intimidate other board members and create a dysfunctional working climate. Some board chairs ask members to fill out an informal evaluation form at the end of each meeting so they can air their concerns about the board process. Be sure to plan for follow-up to address the issues raised.

Personal issues should not be brought into the boardroom, but if these issues have an adverse affect on board performance, the chair must handle the situation with those who are responsible. One chair had to deal with the damaging comments of one board member who questioned the expertise of a board colleague during a discussion. The chair immediately asked the board member to refrain from making personal attacks, and later had a private chat with him about his conduct.

How To Handle a Board Member with a Personal Agenda

What happens when a board member — who also happens to be a major donor — brings a strong personal agenda into the boardroom? Relationship building comes in here. In a private conversation, the board chair needs to listen to the board member's concerns and try to understand the personal agenda and its meaning. With this foundation, you may be able to point out that the person's concerns are already incorporated into the board's agenda or that they warrant further discussion at an executive committee or board meeting. If the board member's own priorities disrupt the board's work, you may need to reinforce the board member role of good stewardship for the entire organization — not just one project or one service — and frame it in the context of good governance.

Sanctioning or Terminating a Board Member

Before a person is elected to serve as a board member, information about board membership responsibilities and standards of conduct should be provided. For example, potential board members are fully entitled to know if there are time requirements other than attendance at board meetings. This may include service on a committee or task force, attendance at special events, or any additional work outside of regular board meetings specific to the organization. It is also important to be up front about the conflict-of-interest policy and its enforcement so a board candidate understands that membership requires the organization's needs taking precedence over personal or professional gains. Every board member should be familiar with the clauses in the bylaws that deal with board member removal.

As board chair, you carry out board policies related to sanctioning or terminating a board member. Violation of policies on such matters as attendance, boundaries, standards of conduct, and conflict of interest require a response. This is one of the toughest tasks faced by a board chair. From a governance perspective, you should approach each situation with an open mind and investigate the allegation to determine what actions need to be taken.

A board member may be sanctioned when he or she puts personal or professional interests ahead of the best interests of the organization. This includes

- using information learned as a board member in a different role outside the boardroom

- lack of diligence in carrying out the work of the board as an informed, engaged board member

- actions based on personal values and beliefs rather than support for the organization's mission and purpose

- not acknowledging a conflict of interest

There is no room for board member impropriety or the perception of impropriety. Acting on board policy, the board chair needs to hold each board member accountable for his or her actions or lack thereof.

If a board member misses too many meetings or does not show commitment to service, other members can become resentful. First, find out whether the board member or the board process is at fault. Is the board member absent because of personal problems that have little or nothing to do with his or her commitment? Or does the board member experience meetings as boring or unproductive with little opportunity for purposeful dialogue? Perhaps he or she does not feel valued and, therefore, does not see the need to attend a meeting.

Since every board member is a legal steward of the organization and is accountable for the work of the board, attendance at board meetings should be mandatory. All members should receive a meeting schedule at the beginning of the board year so they can plan appropriately. Each board must decide how to carry out its attendance policy and recognize the pros and cons of sanctioning a board member. For example, a board that meets every other month could have a policy that a member who misses two board meetings in a row without a reasonable excuse (such as illness or family emergency) may be asked to relinquish his or her board position or be put on notice that he or she may be asked to step down after one more missed meeting. Before enforcing an attendance policy, the chair should meet with the board member to clarify the situation and decide on a course of action. The bylaws should have clear guidelines to allow the board chair to make a fair and just decision on how to proceed.

Board members may have many valid reasons for their inability to attend meetings, including geographic distance and increased professional responsibilities. Regardless of the reason, the board needs to accomplish its work, so the chair may need to take action. Board members who live too far away or are too overwhelmed by other commitments may be able to step down from the board but serve the organization in another capacity — as a committee member or volunteer, for example. Stepping down does not mean stepping out. This, too, is part of board member preservation. (See Appendix 2 for sample letters to board members.)

BOARD CHAIR'S TO DO LIST

- ✓ Be proactive in using the board development model to identify and engage individuals as potential board members, maximize each board member's contributions to the board, and maintain engagement of outgoing board members.

- ✓ Ensure that board development initiatives exist for board member identification, orientation, sustainability, and preservation.

- ✓ Cultivate and sustain relationships with new, ongoing, or terminating board members for optimizing the work of the board.

- ✓ Manage individual and group issues that challenge the healthy functioning of the board.

6.

Generative Thinking and Decision Making

How board decisions are made depends in large part on the leadership of the board chair. People look to the chair as a role model for addressing immediate and long-range concerns in a proactive way. It's up to the board chair to lead the board to "better goals, better questions, and a better sense of problems and opportunities."[6] A decision-making model infused with generative thinking will guide the board in moving the organization forward and achieving *better outcomes*.

GENERATIVE THINKING

The psychologist Erik Erikson, who theorized about child and adult behavior, described the developmental task of middle adulthood as "generativity vs. stagnation." He defined generativity as "concern for establishing and guiding the next generation," which reaches beyond one's immediate, personal needs.[7] According to Erikson, without generativity, there is stagnation, characterized by "interpersonal impoverishment" and an inability to connect outside of oneself. Stagnation represents immobilization — the inability to move forward and thrive.

Richard P. Chait, William P. Ryan, and Barbara E. Taylor present a similar case for organizational generativity. They describe generative thinking as a cognitive process providing a necessary construct for shaping the work of the board and leading to effective board governance. Generative thinking offers a "think tank" framework for moving an organization forward by

We have made great progress over the past five years in advancing from being an operations-focused board to being a strategic board that makes knowledge-driven decisions. This is very challenging, and given that about 40% of our board turns over every year, developing continuity in focus is a particular challenge. But I do think we've become a much more successful organization through transformation of our governance practices, and have generated outcomes (popular new services, more effective advocacy work, more diversified income sources) that would have been unattainable a few years ago.

~ Chief Executive

- identifying all cues and clues to extrapolate meaning;

---

6. Richard P. Chait, William P. Ryan, and Barbara E. Taylor, *Governance as Leadership: Reframing the Work of Nonprofit Boards* (Hoboken, N.J.: John Wiley & Sons, 2005), p. 85.

7. Erik H. Erikson, *Identity: Youth and Crisis* (New York: W.W. Norton, 1968), p. 138.

- adapting multiple organizational frames of reference (such as organizational policies and procedures, human resources, power and politics, and organizational culture); and

- using the past to frame the future.[8]

Generative thinking benefits from the interchange of diverse voices and should be infused in every aspect of board tasks, from setting mission, to solving problems, to setting strategy, to evaluating outcomes. Such a deliberate cognitive process requires the board chair to facilitate dialogue that helps the board analyze and synthesize information from multiple sources. In achieving shared meaning and gaining insights into this material, the board chair should encourage openness to explore multiple frames of reference, from which emerge a range of strategies and options for decision making — hence, better outcomes.

A board chair should encourage generative thinking even when it is not related to specific tasks. William P. Ryan suggests carving out generative space at board

QUESTIONS THAT STIMULATE GENERATIVE THINKING

Chait, Ryan, and Taylor suggest the use of catalytic questions "that invite creativity, exploration, and do not depend largely on data and logic to answer."[9]

- What keeps you awake at night about the organization?

- What are we missing in this discussion?

- How can we frame this situation differently?

- What best explains our recent successes? Our setbacks?

- What headline would we most/least like to see about the organization?

- What is the biggest gap between what the organization claims it is and what it actually is?

- How do we incorporate the organization's core values in our work?

- What is the best possible outcome? The worst-case scenario?

- How would we operate differently as a for-profit organization?

- If you were on the board of a competing organization, what would you do to most effectively compete against us?

---

8. Chait et al., *Governance as Leadership*, 85-88.

9. Chait et al., *Governance as Leadership*, p. 123.

meetings to promote robust discourse.[10] For example, have index cards available at the end of a meeting for members to write down any unfinished or new thoughts and concerns or business not addressed at the meeting. Collect the cards, and raise these points at the beginning of the next meeting. Another idea is to give the chief executive the same opportunity to raise general issues and concerns from his or her perspective.

Generative thinking, as mandatory for good stewardship, supports purposeful board membership and strong, dynamic, healthy organizations. Just as the person in middle adulthood needs to care about the future or risk individual impoverishment and stagnation, so, too, does the organization need to take care of its future or risk organizational impoverishment and stagnation.

A FIVE-STEP DECISION-MAKING MODEL

Situations requiring a thoughtful decision-making process informed by generative thinking include, but are not limited to

- Introducing a new program idea
- Deciding to accept a donation with strings attached
- Responding to a public relations issue
- Considering a new collaboration with a community partner
- Engaging in succession planning
- Deliberating on budget allocations

The board chair can apply the following five-step decision-making model in collaboration with those who are involved in framing a decision, including the chief executive, the full board, and community stakeholders. This model calls for the board chair to apply group facilitation skills and infuse generative thinking in all steps. Diverse board opinions should be heard. Throughout the decision-making process, the board chair should observe participants' reactions and use empathy and confrontation to acknowledge feelings, attitudes, tensions, discrepancies, and what is not being said.

STEP 1. FACT FINDING

Get the facts; don't make assumptions. You may need to talk with one or more individuals or groups to uncover the who, what, where, when, and how of a situation. Fact finding may require gathering information and best practices or comparisons with peer organizations. Give context to the situation by framing it from multiple perspectives. Use communication skills to get specifics and probe for meaning.

---

10. William P. Ryan, "*Governance as Leadership: Practice Applications and Implications,*" presentation at the BoardSource Leadership Forum, Chicago, December 4, 2006.

STEP 2. INFORMATION ASSESSMENT

Once the information is collected, help the board assess what is known. Depending on the issue, assessment may include an analysis of the circumstances surrounding the situation: what brings it to the board's attention now, motives behind it, challenges presented, positive aspects, impact on organization, and what information is missing. Apply multiple perspectives using generative thinking to create an assessment that integrates all the available information and makes note of the gaps. Synthesize what is known to develop a more complete, insightful "big picture."

STEP 3. EXPLORATION OF OPTIONS

Develop multiple response options. What should the outcomes look like? How could they be achieved? How would the outcomes look from different perspectives? Explore the pros and cons of each option, including the potential consequences of choosing one over another. One single outcome may be organized around a central

---

HOW ONE BOARD APPLIED THE FIVE-STEP DECISION-MAKING MODEL

A nonprofit organization's chief executive was offered the opportunity to rent space at another nonprofit's main location to use as a satellite location. Armed with a map of the location and a cost analysis, she brought this option to her board "for approval" and explained why it was a good opportunity for the organization. The board chair facilitated board members' questioning to learn more about this potential arrangement.

Board members viewed the facts from the organization's multiple perspectives (including consumers, community stakeholders, donors, staff resources, and mission fit). They also addressed their questions from the perspective of the other organization (its purpose and need, its potential gain from this arrangement, the impact on its consumers) and considered the political implications in the community. Board members inquired about other options for expanding to a satellite location. What did the bigger expansion picture look like for the organization, and was the presented option the most desirable location?

The board decided that it could not make a quick decision because good stewardship required more information, a discussion of options, and an assessment of how the decision would affect other programs. The board chair appointed an ad hoc committee to study the matter further. After hearing the committee's report, the board decided not to approve the original option, since it did not appear to be in the best interests of the organization. However, the dialogue raised the idea of exploring community outreach options, so the board chair and chief executive suggested a task force of board and staff members to study the possibilities for the board's future consideration.

idea and could incorporate multiple steps or responses. The options can include: public response, private response, board resolution, new task force, marketing plan, e-mail communication, formal letter, program or staff change, governance or board member change, bylaw change, policy modification, new revenue stream, face-to-face meetings, new community partner, new organizational direction, or further deliberations.

STEP 4. OUTCOMES AND ACTION PLAN

Develop consensus around an outcome or outcomes, and create an action plan to achieve it. Good intentions get lost without concreteness and accountability. Questions to consider include: Who is responsible for responding and to whom? How should the response be communicated? What documentation or materials need to be created and distributed? What is the timeframe for responding? What resources (financial, personnel, supplies, etc.) are needed? If the final outcome is further deliberations, return to step 1 of this model, delegated to the appropriate committee or task force.

STEP 5. FOLLOW-UP AND EVALUATION

Conduct any necessary follow-up during the implementation of the action plan to determine the need for modifications or additional response. Evaluate the effectiveness of the action plan and request feedback from all involved parties to assess if the response was appropriate. If you need to make modifications, return to the decision-making model for further deliberations if necessary.

Remember that all outcomes have consequences. As board chair, you should ensure that such outcomes are ethically and legally sound and serve the best interests of the organization.

BOARD CHAIR'S TO DO LIST

✓ Be a generative thinker and ask catalytic questions.

✓ Facilitate robust dialogue at board meetings, and encourage big-picture-thinking.

✓ Infuse generative thinking in board decisions and outcomes.

✓ Use the five-step decision-making model to support thoughtful and thorough board decisions and outcomes.

7.

Board Work Structures

The board chair should be a champion for developing procedures and guidelines that help the board work efficiently and effectively. Having a structure in place for conducting board business

- allows for fluid verbal and written communications;
- maximizes valuable time;
- keeps important matters from falling through the cracks;
- keeps the chief executive and board members informed; and
- shows respect for each person's time and contributions to the organization.

Faced with options for organizing the work of the board, a board chair must decide how to use an executive committee, other committees, task forces, advisory groups, and other resources. The board's existing structure may set a precedent, but perhaps it is time to reevaluate the possibilities for optimizing the board's work. As board chair, you can work with the chief executive and other board members to create and facilitate work structures for the board.

BOARD MEETINGS

As board chair, you are responsible for facilitating effective and efficient board meetings — effective in the sense that the board accomplishes its work with full board member participation and efficient in the sense that each agenda item has a time limit and the meeting ends on time. The chair takes on multiple tasks in meeting this responsibility: planning the meeting agenda (with the chief executive), communicating with board members and committees between board meetings, reporting to the board between meetings as needed, and leading and facilitating the actual board meeting,

The best board meetings are the result of a coordinated effort by board and staff.[11] The board chair and the chief executive set the agenda, carefully thinking through the contents to cover all the board's

---

BOARD SIZE

47% of boards have fewer than 15 voting members

39% have 15 to 22

14% have 23 or more

60% of board members think their board size is fine

24% wisher it were larger

16% wish it were smaller

---

11. Outi Flynn, *Meet Smarter: A Guide to Better Nonprofit Board Meetings* (Washington, D.C.: BoardSource, 2004), p. 4.

business in the allotted amount of time. Be reasonable in determining the length of the agenda. The more agenda items, the longer the meeting, and you will need to allow enough time for board member inquiry and dialogue. As the board's leader, the chair has final approval of the agenda and responsibility for managing it during the meeting. Sample meeting agendas are included in Appendix 2.

The agenda covers three categories:

- *Information items* provide board members with information, knowledge, or data. Examples include committee reports, program updates, and new funding information. No action is required of board members. Instead of listing each information item on the meeting agenda, a consent agenda is used and listed as the board agenda item.

- *Discussion items* share information or pose big-picture, what-if questions and ask for board members' input into the current and future work of the organization. Examples include discussion, assessment, or brainstorming around fundraising ideas; committee work (such as creating a volunteer strategy or a board development plan, exploring governance issues, or generating marketing ideas); community issues; social, political, or economic conditions; and trends, opportunities, and threats in the sector. No further decisions or action are required of board members. Any new ideas, comments, issues, and concerns are applied to the follow-up, in-process work by the full board, committee, task force, or staff member.

- *Action items* convey information, knowledge, or data and ask for a board decision or vote. Examples include voting on the annual budget, setting strategic planning goals, and creating a new program or service. It is critical that any printed material needed for an action item be sent ahead to all board members so they can prepare accordingly.

Depending on how often a board meets and the typical length of a board meeting, the board agenda should reflect a mix of these three categories. If an agenda only lists informational items, there is probably no need for a board meeting!

EXECUTIVE COMMITTEE

An executive committee needs a stated purpose and clear guidelines, usually outlined in the bylaws. Some executive committees meet only in emergencies. Others meet more regularly and are charged with special projects or guiding the board's future work. Some serve as a sounding board for the chief executive. Small boards (fewer than 10 members) or start-up organizations rarely need an executive committee. The board itself would handle all issues as they arise.

> We have an executive session at each meeting to provide an opportunity for the executive and board to discuss issues and concerns without staff. The board meets first with the CEO and then without the CEO at each meeting. The meeting without the CEO provides a peer-to-peer discussion opportunity.
>
> ~ Chief Executive

How To Use a Consent Agenda

A consent agenda is a tool for presenting routine information so that board members do not have to listen to report after report, taking away valuable meeting time. The board chair should explain how the consent agenda works to ensure that it truly enhances the productivity of the meetings.

Committee or task force reports usually are included in the consent agenda. Ahead of time, ask committee chairs to prepare a short summary highlighting current work and focusing on what the board needs to know. If the committee needs the board's assistance or input — volunteers, donated items, community contacts, or other resources — the report should provide details.

Items on a consent agenda often include

1. Approval of board meeting minutes (attach the minutes)

2. Approval of meeting agendas

3. Committee and task force reports

4. Informational material (e.g., volunteer of the month, recent newspaper articles, community survey, trend sector report)

5. Routine correspondence specific to the organization (e.g., list of grants and contracts)

6. Special events (e.g., reports on fundraising events, dates of upcoming events, list of community events)

7. Confirmation of minute changes to key documents (e.g., corrections of typing errors in bylaws or changed addresses)

The composition depends on the board structure and the committee's purpose. For example, an executive committee called together in emergency situations may need members who can easily get to a meeting location. Another board's executive committee may consist of board officers and meet more regularly.

EXECUTIVE SESSIONS

The board chair has the right and responsibility to call for executive sessions when confidential or otherwise sensitive issues need to be discussed. The purpose of the session determines who is present and who is excluded. The chief executive may participate in them or no staff may be in the room during the session.

When an Executive Committee Gets Off Track

If a board tends to act like a rubber-stamp board, the executive committee is probably wielding too much power and taking on tasks that the full board should be handling. The executive committee should supplement and support the board's work, not the other way around. The power and authority of the executive committee should never take the place of or exceed the power and authority of the board.

As board chair, you should be alert to this problem and may need to enlist the support of the governance committee or a special task force to bring about change. Be attentive to signs of board member disengagement:

- Low board attendance

- Reduced or flat financial contributions

- Disinterest in board decisions

- Lack of follow-through on other commitments or responsibilities

If the executive committee appears to be usurping the role of the board, the board chair should check this perception with other board members. What is the purpose of the executive committee? Is the board too large for carrying out its role? Remember that all board members are legally responsible and accountable for the work of the board — not just those on the executive committee. If necessary, introduce a recommendation to reassess the purpose of the executive committee and/or reduce the size of the board.

According to BoardSource, the following situations are suitable for an executive session[12]:

- Discussion of financial issues with an auditor

- Preparation for a case with a lawyer

- Exploration of planning for major business or strategic endeavors, such as mergers or real estate deals

- Discussion of the board's approach to a scandal or negative publicity

- Handling of personnel issues, such as chief executive compensation, performance evaluation, or disciplinary issues

- Handling of any matters where confidentiality has been requested or is otherwise prudent or legally required

- Peer-to-peer discussions about board operations

---

12. BoardSource, "Executive Sessions: How To Use Them Regularly and Wisely," (BoardSource, 2007) p. 2; www.boardsource.org

When instituting an executive session, the chair needs to ensure its proper use. Discuss only what the session is called for and inform the chief executive (if not present) and the board of the results afterward. Make sure any meeting notes or minutes remain confidential.

COMMITTEES AND TASK FORCES

The board chair, in partnership with the chief executive, ensures that every board committee or task force has a clear purpose of what needs to be accomplished. With input from the chief executive and board members, the chair is responsible for appointing committee chairs as needed. Depending on the organization, the task of identifying committee members may fall to the chair and chief executive, other board members, or the committee chair.

The four most common standing committees reported are executive, finance, governance/nominating, and fundraising/development. Your organization's bylaws should outline standing committees and procedures for creating ad hoc committees or task forces. The board chair can appoint a task force or an ad hoc committee as needed to address a time-limited task with a specific objective, such as

---

Which committees do boards have?

Executive (79%)

Finance (77%)

Governance/Nominating (68%)

Fundraising/Development (57%)

Audit (40%)

---

strategic planning, public relations campaign, or study group for future program expansion. Keep in mind that board committee structure is not set in stone — these smaller work groups should reflect the needs of the board and the organization,[13] and one size does not fit all, although some committees may be mandated by state laws governing nonprofits or by a national umbrella organization.

As board chair, you need to ensure there is communication with your committee and task force chairs in order to keep the board informed. As mentioned earlier, use the consent agenda as a tool for providing updates. Since most committee work involves board and staff members, the board chair and the chief executive should see to it that there is a policy for board-staff communications. Board members should be clear on what and how to communicate with staff in order to encourage appropriate communications and not undermine the authority of the chief executive or another staff member.

RETREATS

A board retreat dedicates time for board members and selected staff to explore issues, trends, and challenges that may affect the work of the board or the organization. Since a retreat is a work structure of the board, the chair should be involved in the planning process, which a special task force or committee may spearhead. You should

---

13. Marla J. Bobowick, Sandra R. Hughes, and Berit M. Lakey, *Transforming Board Structure: Strategies for Committees and Task Forces* (Washington, D.C.: BoardSource, 2001), p. 12.

communicate clearly to board members the purpose and objectives of the retreat and the importance of each member's participation to the successful outcome.

According to Sandra Hughes, a board retreat can produce a range of benefits:

- An opportunity for planning and team building that the pressure of regular board activities simply won't allow

- A chance to refocus on fundamentals; engage in thoughtful strategic planning; and reflect on mission, vision, and strategic goals

- A vehicle for strengthening trust and relationships among board members and between board and staff, or for pulling together a divided board on a critical issue

- A time to conduct or respond to a board self-assessment[14]

One board chair shared the importance of a board retreat held after a restructuring that brought on a significant number of new members. The retreat was an opportunity to conduct a board orientation along with a visioning exercise to which each member contributed. The final vision statement was printed on the back of the name cards used at board meetings as a constant reminder of the board's hopes and expectations for the year.

BOARD COMMUNICATION LINKAGES

Board communications relate to any potential or actual issues, trends, risks, challenges, and items connected to board stewardship and the work of the organization. A strong board structure requires well-established and clear communication channels and a board chair who is willing to confront communication obstacles. Keeping board members "in the loop" is crucial to ensuring the best possible board performance. As board chair, your goal is to plan and manage the logistics and content of communication flow.

When the chief executive or a committee chair shares information, the board chair needs to monitor board members' responses and the need for additional information. As the contact person for board members, you will help channel information between the board and the chief executive or committee chair when board members have questions about what is presented and discussed at a board meeting. The board chair needs to allow board members to communicate to him or her so that the chair, in consort with the chief executive, can figure out how to provide better information.

The following questions will help you evaluate and facilitate communication flow:

- How does the board structure affect communication flow?

- How are smaller work structures, such as committees and task forces, accountable to the full board? Are certain board members or executive committee members designated communication links?

---

14. Sandra R. Hughes, *To Go Forward, Retreat! The Board Retreat Handbook* (Washington, D.C.: BoardSource, 1999), p. 7.

- How is information shared with the full board?

- Are board members receiving information in a timely manner?

- Does the communication flow accommodate information from multiple directions, not just top down?

- How does the board monitor external communication linkages with community stakeholders and other organizations?

The board's governance committee can be responsible for assessing board communications. Sometimes an ad hoc committee or task force has this assignment. In the interest of creating and sustaining an effective board process, it is up to the chair to ensure that board communication linkages are in place.

BOARD CHAIR'S TO DO LIST

✓ Choose work structures that optimize the work of the board.

✓ Create meeting agendas that respect the available time and the purpose of the board.

✓ Use a consent agenda for disseminating information that does not require discussion or an immediate board vote.

✓ Keep the board informed and ensure fluid and appropriate communication.

✓ Address, don't ignore, obstacles limiting effective board communications.

8.

Resource Development and Fiscal Oversight

An umbrella association of nonprofit family and children's services organizations polled its members' board chairs to learn what their most pressing concerns were. Overwhelmingly, most of these leaders responded with one word: fundraising. An organization must frame any fundraising activity in the larger context of fiduciary responsibility, board policies, and organizational mission.

RESOURCE DEVELOPMENT

The term *resource development* describes the range of options available to an organization for increasing funds to deliver, sustain, and expand its programs and services. It may encompass a membership or annual campaign, capital campaign, endowments, foundation grants, individual donors, and special fundraising events. Many nonprofit organizations have a development director or office that coordinates these activities. A resource development or fundraising committee coordinates board members' engagement in fundraising and helps draft board member giving and organizational gift-acceptance policies.

There are eight ways board members can be involved in resource development:

> **Board members expressed the most comfort with writing and/or signing personal solicitation letters (69%) and providing names/addresses for solicitation letters (59%). Only 40% feel comfortable making phone calls to potential donors and only 36% feel comfortable asking for money directly. About half (51%) feel comfortable meeting face-to-face with donors.**

- Identify resource needs during the strategic planning process.

- Help create a strategic resource development plan.

- Use personal contacts to expand the organization's resource base.

- Identify and evaluate potential donors.

- Cultivate potential donors.

- Write and send annual solicitation letters.

- Organize and host special fundraising events.

- Write thank-you notes to donors.[15]

---

15. BoardSource, *Presenting: Fund-Raising — The Board Member's Role in Resource Development* (Washington, D.C., BoardSource, 2002), p. 4.

FUNDRAISING REQUIREMENTS

Boards require their board members to participate in fundraising in a variety of ways:

Making a personal monetary contribution (61%)

Identifying donors (56%)

Attending fundraising events (54%)

Soliciting funds (46%)

As board chair, you work closely with the chief executive, the development office, and the board's development committee to maximize the board's role in resource development. Along with other key players, you will mobilize board members to participate. Above all, you are a role model to other board members in terms of financial support of the organization, attendance at fundraising and membership events, donor cultivation, gift solicitation, and other activities.

Some organizations set a minimum expected contribution, while some do not dictate a minimum. Other organizations encourage board members to contribute to a particular sponsored function (such as an annual conference or awards dinner) or to attend certain fundraising events. Either you or a member of the development committee may be asking board members for their support. Regardless, you need to reinforce development efforts at board meetings and with individual board members

---

TIPS FOR SOLICITING BOARD MEMBER CONTRIBUTIONS

- Make your financial contribution before asking others.

- Announce the membership campaign or special event to the board, and tell board members to expect a personal call from you.

- Remind the board that each member is required to make a financial contribution in support of the organization.

- Choose personal meetings or phone calls over e-mail or a letter, but consider a follow-up letter confirming the conversation. This can serve to provide documentation of the discussion. (A sample letter can be found in Appendix 2.)

- Frame the "ask" as a responsibility and a privilege, acknowledging the importance of 100 percent board participation.

- Reinforce that board members' financial support allows the organization to continue offering quality programs and services in meeting the community's needs.

- Acknowledge the member for the work and time he or she has contributed.

- Don't be afraid to ask for an increase over last year's donation (if there is a giving history).

- Thank the member for his or her donation, regardless of the amount.

- Follow up with a handwritten note after the contribution is received.

as needed. One board chair likes to tell his board, "Give until it feels great!"

The board chair should ensure that each board member has a role in helping to meet the fundraising goals. Some may say they do not like fundraising and do not do it well, but everyone should be involved on some level. Many boards provide training sessions before the start of a fundraising effort or membership campaign. Those few members who do not end up making solicitations can be engaged in other tasks.

As board chair, you might accompany the development director or chief executive when he or she is cultivating a major donor or making a solicitation. Some donors or funders may request to meet the board chair, or the organization may initiate an introduction when building new donors and funders. You should help the development director and chief executive assess what you bring to the table, including

- the status associated with the board chair position;

- personal and professional contacts;

- a background in finance or resource development;

- the ability to cultivate relationships;

- commitment to and passion for the organization; and

- representation of the board's commitment to a specific program or campaign.

FISCAL OVERSIGHT

Resource development falls under the overarching function of the board's fiscal oversight of the organization. The board has fiduciary responsibility to

- ensure financial integrity and solvency;

- ensure that safeguards and procedures are in place to protect the organization;

- ensure that signs of financial trouble are recognized and acted on;

- ensure that financial practices follow defined state and federal laws; and

- ensure that an annual financial audit is conducted, when appropriate.[16]

When appropriate, the board will be asked to deliberate on and approve a budget in the framework of providing programs and services aligned with organizational mission. It is the chair's job to recognize the competition for resources and to make sure that the board follows established priorities when making budget decisions.

---

16. Andrew S. Lang, *Financial Responsibilities of Nonprofit Boards*, rev. ed. (Washington, D.C.: BoardSource, 2003), p. vii.

Once the board has agreed to the mission and has set the organization's strategic priorities, any conflict over allocation of resources must be resolved by testing to see if the budget matches up with those priorities. The time to make those decisions is when the budget is approved, not weeks or months later. As board chair, you must ensure that the finance committee, in working with the chief executive or chief financial officer, provides complete budget information and issues to board members for review prior to board deliberations. You may also choose to have input into budget discussions at finance committee meetings.

The board chair needs to make certain that every board member is educated on fiscal matters and, if necessary, ask the board treasurer and the organization's chief financial officer to conduct a board training session before the board makes budget decisions. Board education related to fiduciary responsibilities and current financial practices should be ongoing and customized to the needs of the board.

It is imperative to practice fiscal transparency related to budget, investment strategies, donor funds, vendor contracts, and all organizational purchases and expenses. The organization's policies and procedures, in consort with those individuals responsible for financial matters, should support fiscal transparency. Any fiscal misconduct by senior staff or board members must be dealt with as soon as the chair learns of the situation. Depending on the source of the misconduct, the board chair may need to initiate an executive session, engage the finance committee, seek outside counsel, or hire an auditor.

BOARD CHAIR'S TO DO LIST

✓ Be a role model and engage the board in resource development activities, which include providing financial support to the organization, attending fundraising events, identifying and cultivating donors, and making solicitations.

✓ In coordination with the chief executive and the development officer, be available as an asset in resource development activities.

✓ Help to educate and engage board members to ensure sound fiscal oversight of the organization.

9.

Strategic and Program Planning

The board chair ensures that the organization is accountable to its mission by engaging the board in strategic and program planning initiatives. Together with the chief executive, you need to assess current status and set the agenda for these tasks.

STRATEGIC PLANNING

Strategic planning (also known as *visioning*) offers a formal process for examining what actions are necessary to move an organization forward, usually over two to three years. Strategic planning seeks to align internal operations with external exigencies in developing strategic goals along with action plans to achieve them. The resulting plan provides a framework for the chief executive and staff in meeting organizational mission. There are different strategic planning models, and some organizations emphasize creating strategic priorities over a more formal plan.

In partnership, the board chair and chief executive are responsible for ensuring that the organization has a strategic plan. A board chair may help to initiate a new strategic plan, monitor an ongoing one, or evaluate a plan coming to conclusion. Working with the chief executive, you should determine what strategic planning steps need to be undertaken during your term of office.

Many organizations hire an outside consultant to facilitate the critical task of strategic planning. The consultant usually works with a committee or task force of board and staff members that coordinates the overall planning effort. A board member or perhaps the incoming chair, if identified, can chair the committee. The mix of board and staff perspectives gives board members a better understanding of day-to-day issues while helping staff appreciate longer-term concerns.[17]

A BASIC STRATEGIC PLANNING MODEL

A plethora of books are available for guidance in developing a strategic plan. For the board's role, the basic steps in a strategic planning process include

- **Develop or reaffirm mission statement.**

  Strategic planning flows from mission. The board should periodically review and revise the mission statement, along with the vision statement or core values. The board chair's role: Facilitate board discussion to ensure mission and vision statements reflect the work of the organization; appoint a task force if needed for further study.

---

17. Deborah L. Kocsis and Susan A. Waechter, *Driving Strategic Planning: A Nonprofit Executive's Guide* (Washington, D.C.: BoardSource, 2003), p. 13.

- Conduct an internal organizational assessment.

  Review and analyze the organization's operations, services, and programs related to process and outcomes, and create a profile of strengths and weaknesses. The board chair's role: Oversee this step through an objective third party; help identify areas for review.

- Conduct an environmental scan.

  Review and analyze opportunities, challenges, and trends that may affect the organization's work. Invite community input from a variety of stakeholders. The board chair's role: Work with the chief executive to identify community stakeholders; have input into framing the questions.

- Examine strategic issues.

  Address the interplay between internal and external assessments and their actual and potential impact on the organization. Identify strategic issues to consider. If necessary, reexamine and revise the mission statement. The board chair's role: Assist the board in understanding the assessment results and their impact through the lens of the organization's mission; engage the board in robust dialogue to identify challenges and opportunities.

- Formulate strategic goals and priorities.

  In some organizations, the strategic planning committee develops a draft for board discussion. Other boards work collectively to develop goals and priorities. Ultimately, the full board must deliberate and vote on a final list. The board chair's role: Facilitate board discussion around strategic directions; ensure consensus with the final strategic goals or priorities.

- Create action plans.

  Some boards delegate this task to staff, while others may work collaboratively with staff through task forces or work groups. The board chair's role: Ask each board member to serve on a task force to assist in the creation of an action plan.

- Monitor and evaluate implementation of the strategic plan.

  Implementing the strategic plan is the staff's responsibility, under the chief executive, while monitoring and evaluating it is the board's responsibility. The board chair's role: Ensure that the board receives periodic strategic plan progress reports and evaluations of the implementation process.

PROGRAM PLANNING AND EVALUATION

The board makes decisions about how to use resources and set goals (program planning), and it evaluates whether resources are used effectively and goals are achieved (program evaluation). Program planning and evaluation are an active partnership between staff and board. Professional staff is responsible for carrying out program activities and it is important to define an appropriate process for the board's involvement. Depending on board size and frequency of meetings, the board may routinely handle programmatic issues as a part of a well-planned agenda, or the chair may need to appoint a committee or task force to assist in carrying out these responsibilities when more detailed assessment at the board level is necessary.

PROGRAM PLANNING

The chair would lead the board to focus on present and new programs. The discussions would help identify new program initiatives (for example, community outreach, opening a new service center, global expansion) and provide input into expanding, reducing, or eliminating existing programs and services. During these deliberations, the chair should ensure that the board pays attention to the following priorities:

- Stay on course with the strategic plan.

- Evaluate all initiatives against the mission and values of the organization.

HELPING BOARD MEMBERS LEARN ABOUT PROGRAMS

Together the board chair and chief executive should make sure that board members are knowledgeable about the organization's programs and services. This educational component can be incorporated in a board meeting or outside the board room. Some examples include:

- staff presentation at a board meeting

- visit to a program site

- e-mail educational update

- consent agenda item report

- board manual material

- leadership training opportunity outside the board meeting

- board retreat.

Be creative in finding ways to develop knowledgeable board members. One board chair took her board members on a "road trip" to visit the various sites where the organization provided programs and services. Board members boarded a bus at one location and toured the community to three other sites. At each site, staff members presented information and responded to participant questions (clients were not in attendance to respect confidentiality). After the tour, board members returned to the first site for a communal dinner and a chance to share their reflections on the road trip. They gained a different perspective on the organization from this firsthand experience, which had a positive effect on their program planning and evaluation decisions.

- Ensure that the constituents are well served.

- Make sure that adequate funding and other resources are available for quality programs.

- Investigate what other peer organizations — competitors — are doing and whether collaboration is possible.

- Remain on top of industry and sector trends.

Productive board involvement in program planning involves thinking beyond the status quo. The board chair should encourage generative thinking about new program ideas or modifications to existing programs. The "big picture" context — community and sector trends and challenges — should be addressed in reinforcing strong stewardship.

PROGRAM EVALUATION

Program evaluation is one way a nonprofit organization assesses its success at fulfilling its mission. Both output data (which measure such variables as number of people served and number of programs offered) and outcomes data (which measure program effectiveness) have become the norm. The board uses this data to inform the following activities:

- Budgeting and fundraising

- Strategic planning

- Public relations/marketing strategy

- Board member recruitment

- Community collaborations

- Chief executive evaluation

- Further program planning

- Organizational mission alignment or reassessment

The board chair should ensure that the chief executive and staff are conducting outcomes evaluations with the right tools and enough resources. It is critical that the evaluation results do not sit on a shelf, but are applied in board decision making. An evaluation may reveal that a program is surprisingly ineffective, but it may be a fixture in the organization, or a donor's special interest, or a staff favorite. Nevertheless, the evaluation results indicate that the board should disband or retool it. The challenge for the board chair is to emphasize process and facilitate a board discussion that explores all the variables framed for the good of the organization.

BOARD CHAIR'S TO DO LIST

✓ Ensure that the organization has a strategic plan.

✓ Oversee the hiring of a strategic planning consultant, if needed.

✓ Facilitate board communications around strategic planning.

✓ Maintain momentum in moving the strategic planning process forward, and match board engagement to the current strategic planning tasks.

✓ Encourage generative thinking in brainstorming new program ideas and initiatives.

✓ Work with the chief executive to create opportunities to educate the board about current programs and services.

✓ Apply program evaluation results to board decisions to expand, reduce, or eliminate existing programs and services.

10.

Performance Evaluation

The board's responsibility to monitor organizational progress falls into two categories: performance evaluations and program evaluations (see chapter 9). Leading the performance evaluation process can be challenging for a board chair — not only because it is complex, but also because the results must be implemented in a way that may alter board culture. Evaluation is about being open to constructive feedback to assess how a task, work group, process, skill, behavior, or attitude can be improved upon. The results require appropriate dissemination and study, and then implementation of needed changes depending on who or what is being evaluated. Moreover, evaluation should be a regular activity.

> It's very hard to work for a group of people. Someone always disagrees with you. Sometimes I think this is my dream job, and on other days I think it is clearly time to leave. I think more and more directors have this problem.
>
> ~ Chief Executive

A board chair should ensure that two important performance evaluations are conducted: a board assessment and a chief executive evaluation. Boards may also conduct board chair and individual board member self-evaluations and evaluations of board and committee meetings. Regular performance evaluations have the potential to

- identify issues that are pushed aside during the normal course of business;

- identify strengths and weaknesses that affect optimal performance of the board, an individual, or a work group;

- keep the board and organization focused and on track;

- allow individuals (chief executive, board chair, board members) to assess their growth and progress in their respective roles;

- reinvigorate individual board members to take responsibility as part of a team working toward optimizing board effectiveness; and

- reinforce that the board takes its work seriously and models good governance practices.

BOARD ASSESSMENT

Ongoing monitoring and periodic self-evaluation encourage the board's effectiveness in overseeing and guiding the organization. A proactive board not only monitors itself, but looks to initiate change based on the findings. The frequency of board self-evaluation can vary. A brief annual assessment takes into account that board composition usually shifts each year, affecting board dynamics and board functioning. A more extensive assessment should be conducted every two to four years, looking at

How To Evaluate the Board Chair's Performance

Boards need to be accountable in all areas, including the board chair position. The board chair should receive feedback on how to modify his or her performance to best achieve a high-functioning board. Although a challenge when dealing with a volunteer lay leader, a board chair evaluation framed within the best interests of the organization can be useful.

Like with any evaluation, the process of assessing the chair's performance gives the chair a clearer view of this leadership position and specific requirements to get the job done in the best possible manner. Evaluation clarifies what works and where improvement is desired. It can focus on the chair's facilitation skills, relationships and interactions with board members, use of board work structures, and governance practices. It allows the chair to see how his or her approach to chairing meetings, communication style, and serving as an example is perceived by his or her peers. A board chair evaluation can also help a board avoid informal mumblings or "behind the back" discussions that blur the line between truth and fiction and negatively impact on the work of the board.

The chair evaluation is to be handled by fellow board members. It never is the responsibility of the chief executive. It rarely is an easy task for peers to evaluate each others' performance; therefore, special tact is necessary. Often the task is delegated to the executive committee (or, if one does not exist, to the governance committee). The committee may or may not seek comments from others on the board. Keeping the process anonymous allows everyone to provide as honest and straightforward feedback as possible. The overall comments are communicated directly to the chair in a private discussion. This discussion can also help the chair redirect a course of action if it is necessary.

board composition, structure, operations, committee structure, and roles and responsibilities.

The board chair can delegate the board assessment task to the governance committee or an ad hoc committee. However, a more extensive board assessment may benefit from the services of an outside consultant who has no stake in the outcome.

Keeping an eye on board process (the means) contributes to stronger board outcomes (the end). As board chair, you should engage in board assessment and show initiative in putting the recommended changes into practice. Approaching evaluation in partnership with board members acknowledges each person's stake in and responsibility for becoming a high-performing board. Each person, including the board chair, can reflect on individual contributions and evaluate his or her performance as a board member. This, too, can be part of the annual board assessment.

CHIEF EXECUTIVE EVALUATION

As much as the board chair and chief executive must work in partnership, the reality is that the chief executive works at the pleasure of the board. The chief executive — the only staff member whose performance is assessed by the board — is responsible for the work of the entire staff and the organization's ability to meet its goals. He or she is entitled to receive an annual performance review in order to gauge his or her professional growth in alignment with the organization's direction.

Conducting an annual evaluation of the chief executive is a board responsibility organized by the board chair, who is the volunteer leader with the most direct contact with the chief executive. The board chair could work with the executive committee or a few select board members to conduct this evaluation. The board should have an evaluation process in place with clearly articulated roles for the board chair, other board members, and staff, as appropriate.

There should be congruence between the chief executive's job description, previously set annual goals, and the performance evaluation instrument. Standard forms are available that could be adapted for the organization.[18] A timeframe outlining the steps to be taken can be helpful. The evaluation should be conducted at the end of the fiscal year, when results are in and a new cycle of organizational goals may emerge, necessitating new goals for the chief executive. Frequent and open, formal and informal, communications between the chair and the chief executive are ways to prevent major problems from surfacing out of nowhere. Also helpful is reinforcing ongoing feedback from other board members that is communicated by you to the chief executive in a timely manner.

> ### EVALUATIONS
>
> **52% of boards have conducted a formal, written evaluation of their own performance in the last 12 months**
>
> **16% haven't done so for at least three years**
>
> **74% of boards conduct an annual, formal, written evaluation of the chief executive**

Before meeting with the chief executive to review the evaluation results, share the results with the full board in an executive session to ensure that each board member is familiar with, and ideally agrees with, the final report. The report presents aggregate data and examples to support the performance ratings used to strengthen the executive's functioning, support salary and benefit decisions, and inform contract negotiations. It is also a place to solicit suggestions for performance goals for the next year to be communicated by the chair to the chief executive. The chief executive can choose to incorporate them in writing his or her performance goals for the next year, before they are brought back to the board for approval.

---

18. Joshua Mintz and Jane Pierson, *Assessment of the Chief Executive*, rev. ed. (Washington, D.C.: BoardSource, 2005) and Barbara Lawrence and Outi Flynn, *The Nonprofit Policy Sampler*, 2nd ed. (Washington D.C.: BoardSource, 2006).

Board Chair's To Do List

✓ Ensure that the board conducts a board assessment, reviews the results, and implements change as needed.

✓ Conduct an annual performance evaluation of the chief executive and provide feedback supported by evidence and examples.

✓ Consider ways to obtain feedback about your performance as board chair.

✓ Decide what other evaluations to implement in support of the board's performance.

Part III

The Finale: Creating Endings and New Beginnings

These two chapters explore the end of the journey for a board chair.

- Chapter 11 discusses the need for board chair succession planning, an important process that involves the current chair. The first steps in succession planning may take place much earlier — during the foundation phase when a board chair is building individual capacity. How you end your term as board chair is just as important as how you began. Do you remember the nervous energy and excitement of wanting to do the right thing that drove you to plan ahead and put your best foot forward?

- Chapter 12 explores the idea of bringing closure to your term, a task that also requires focus and energy. Then it's time to ask yourself, "What's next?"

11.

Succession Planning

Succession planning is an ongoing activity for every board, because it should always be a priority to identify and nurture promising leaders. The governance committee, board chair, chief executive, and board members should all have succession planning on their minds. The process is especially crucial for the board chair position. At least by the time the board chair has completed the first half of his or her term, there should be steps taken to identify potential candidates as the next chair. Some boards create a chair-elect position to help make the transition, but there are pitfalls as well as benefits associated with that choice. The current board chair can work closely with a chair-elect to groom him or her for the position, but, on the other hand, taking on the responsibility of a chair-elect prior to being board chair can be a considerable burden.

> Our governance committee has done a great job of board recruitment and development, but we are having great difficulty convincing appropriate board members to ascend to chair. Because our past chairs have been so effective, current board members believe that it is a more time-consuming responsibility than it actually is. We have some great potential candidates, but they are all adamant about not having the time to undertake the responsibility.
>
> ~ Chief Executive

Ideally, the next board chair should be a current board member. It takes time to get to know someone's potential and interest and, on the flip side, for a person to get to know an organization and the role of the board chair. With a strong board development plan and an engaged board, each board member will have leadership opportunities — in committees, task forces, and resource development activities, for example — that will allow for identification and assessment of emerging leaders. The board chair may have informal discussions with individual board members to explore their potential and assess their interest. The self-reflection questions in chapter 1 could be a useful guide. Keep in mind that simply because a board member serves on the executive committee or chairs a committee does not mean that he or she wants to be a future board chair, nor does it mean that he or she would be a good fit.

In some circumstances, a board chair may not come from the board. An organization with financial challenges or a board that is not meeting its stewardship responsibilities may have to look outside the board for a new chair. The chief executive may need to work with funders, individual donors, past board chairs, and community stakeholders to identify new leadership talent.

What if a board chair has been identified but is unable to take on the responsibility due to unforeseen events? If a strong board development plan is in place, there should be depth in the available lineup of future board leaders. If not, the board chair should help the governance committee in identifying someone to succeed him or her.

WHEN THE BOARD CHAIR HAS SERVED TOO LONG

When there is no succession planning, an organization can face a dilemma — what to do about the board chair who has served too long. Organizations with founding board chairs also deal with this scenario. No chair should remain in the leadership role indefinitely. Every organization benefits from fresh ideas and a change in power and authority. The job can take a toll, and the chair's effectiveness may decrease and, in fact, affect the organization's ability to move forward. Asking a long-serving board chair to leave the position is a delicate task regardless of the person's capabilities. Even a successful long-serving board chair needs to step aside in support of building leadership capacity. The role of board chair revolves around what's best for the organization, not what's best for the individual. The bylaws should specify term limits and the orderly transfer of power. Find alternative tasks for the founding or long-term board chair that add value to the board and the organization. Respect his or her contributions and commitment to the organization and, at the same time, reframe new roles for the future.

MENTORING THE CHAIR-ELECT

As you reach the end of your term as board chair, you can be a valuable resource for your successor. In mentoring the next board chair, the outgoing chair can address some of the following topics (keep it professional, not personal):

- Role and responsibilities of the board chair

- Challenging issues that emerged during your tenure

- Unfinished board business

- Status of strategic plan and future trends

- Partnership with the chief executive

- Building relationships with board members, community leaders, donors, and significant others

- Balancing competing demands on one's time

- Big-picture issues

- Communications

- Good governance practices

Many organizations invite the incoming board chair to participate in the regular meetings or phone conferences between the current chair and the chief executive during the months leading up to becoming board chair. The two leaders may have different personalities and leadership styles, and so the issues facing the new chair may be different. Variables such as gender, professional expertise, and age might come into play. The issues facing the organization may demand a fresh assessment and possibly a different approach.

Sometimes an organization will use other approaches for orienting a new board chair, especially if the current board chair doesn't have the time or the inclination to be a mentor. The new chair can gain knowledge, skills, and support through seminars or workshops; online and print resources; community resources; guidance from other board chairs; and coaching and mentoring from a consultant. An investment in developing a board chair who displays strong leadership skills and governance practices can benefit an organization for years to come.

> We are transitioning the board and selecting new members of a higher caliber. We are ensuring that all members selected are true leaders who can inspire or move others to support the organization. Because our process has become much more selective, it has gotten somewhat more difficult. Despite these hurdles, we have been able to attract a very diverse and committed board.
>
> ~ Chief Executive

Another way to help: Share this book with the next board chair!

BOARD CHAIR'S TO DO LIST

✓ Contribute to succession planning by identifying and assessing future leaders.

✓ Be available to mentor the incoming board chair and help with the leadership transition.

✓ Consider a range of other options for mentoring an incoming board chair.

12.

Reaching Closure, Looking Ahead, and Reflecting on the Experience

As your term comes to an end, it's time to complete the transition to a new board chair, reflect on what you've accomplished, and consider what's next in your relationship with the organization. Begin by taking care of some specific things that will bring your work as chair to a satisfying finish.

- **Bring tasks to closure.**

  Let the board and the incoming board chair know where the board's work stands at the end of your tenure. Some tasks remain unfinished, others are completed, and new tasks have been identified. A document that includes committee and task force summaries and a strategic planning report can be useful for your successor, the chief executive, and the board. It also helps to include a big-picture overview that you and the chief executive prepare. With this documentation in hand, everyone is on the same page in moving forward.

- **Bring relationships to closure.**

  A board chair has worked in partnership with the chief executive, staff, board members, and others to create success. Thanking everyone is important in validating and valuing their contributions to the work of the board and the organization. You can thank individuals in conversations, in handwritten notes, or with a donation on their behalf to your organization's "tribute" funds. Or you can take them to lunch or sponsor refreshments at your final board meeting. Don't forget to thank significant others for their support as well.

  Take the time and make the effort to thank each board member and the board as a whole. It is important to let them know that you are grateful for how they give their time, lend their expertise, provide leadership, show passion and commitment, and extend resources on behalf of the organization. Their work as a team — people as process — is what makes for a high-performing board, and they should be commended.

> Our board includes bankers, lawyers, advocates, retirees, human service workers, and 50 percent low-income consumers of our services. We have enormous respect for each other, and meetings are rewarding, thoughtful, often full of laughter, and always focused on the mission. I wish I could bottle this attitude.
>
> ~ Board Member

Other relationships — such as funders, individual donors, and community stake-holders — may also require closure. It is important for these individuals to know that your term is ending. If possible, introduce them to the incoming chair.

- **Reflect on the board's accomplishments.**

  A board discussion of accomplishments gives each board member a chance to reflect individually and collectively on successes and challenges. What is the legacy of this board under the current leadership? Other board members' terms may be ending too, and this exercise provides closure for them.

- **Share self-reflections and board accomplishments with others.**

  As board chair, you should want to share beyond the confines of the boardroom what has been accomplished. You could speak at the annual meeting or in another appropriate venue, or you could write a piece for the organization's newsletter, Web site, or annual report. The board chair and the chief executive could be co-authors of the piece, reinforcing their partnership and emphasizing shared responsibilities.

LOOK TO THE FUTURE

Every board chair wants to step aside graciously to allow his or her successor to take the helm. This gesture is about letting go of the board chair's power and authority to lead and framing a new relationship with the organization. Let the new chair know of your interest and availability to serve the organization, and then distance yourself as he or she rightfully establishes his or her own domain. To do so is a sign of respect and support for succession planning.

Some organizations have designated roles for their immediate past chairs to keep them involved in a different capacity. There may be a term-limited slot on the board as immediate past chair or perhaps membership on an honorary board or advisory group. Whether serving on the board or off the board, your possible roles may include governance committee chair, special event chair, strategic planning committee member, mentor, or advisor.

REFLECT ON YOUR PERSONAL EXPERIENCE

I began this book by talking about the importance of building individual capacity and using it to optimize the work of the board. As you leave the board chair position, it is time to reflect on the experience and explore how it has affected your own growth. Consider what knowledge and skills you have developed, and build on this leadership experience as you decide what to do next and how to use your individual capacity, whether within or outside the organization. Ask yourself the following questions.

As an individual:

- What have I learned about myself from this experience?

- What did I like and dislike about being a leader? How does this information fit with who I am?

- What have I learned about human relationships?

- What have I learned about my community?

- How has this experience affected who I am?

- How has it affected my personal and professional lives?

- How has it affected my relationships with others?

- How can I use my new knowledge and skills in other parts of my life?

As a board chair:

- What are my strengths and weaknesses as a leader?

- How would I assess my work relationships with the chief executive, board members, donors, and other stakeholders?

- How did I contribute to the board and the organization?

- Do I want to stay engaged with the organization? If so, how can I continue to contribute?

- How do I feel about taking on roles and tasks with less power and authority?

- How can I help the new chair without being seen as interfering in his or her work?

- How do I move on after so many years of involvement with this organization?

- How can I share my board chair experiences with other individuals or organizations?

> When I first joined the board, things were pretty much in disarray — problems with the chief executive, lazy recruitment, no orientation, and serious financial problems not shared with the board. Since then, we have restructured our recruitment and orientation but have a ways to go to provide quality training for all board members. We have stronger leadership on the board now and have begun to look strategically to the future, to seriously evaluate the CEO and support and encourage him, and to restructure committees. There is more open discussion, though some "rubber stamping" is still evident. I am very proud of the growth that has occurred over the years.
>
> ~ Board Member

LEAVING A LEGACY

As you reflect on the board's accomplishments during your tenure and on your own contributions as board chair, ideally you will conclude that the organization has benefited. Leaving a legacy is about framing one's work in building organizational capacity for the good of the organization. Your accomplishments may include, but are not limited to

- New program initiatives (such as expanded service areas, a new program, or elimination of an outdated program)

- New processes (such as board assessment, program evaluation, volunteer recruitment, and governance education)

- New community partners

- New donors

- A strong board

To paraphrase John Carver, quality must be perpetually redefined, since what constitutes and defines quality is ever changing and will always remain slightly beyond our grasp.[19] During any board chair's term, achievements are built on the previous chair's legacy and, in turn, will be the foundation for the next chair. Your legacy recognizes that your work has been completed, made a difference, informs the next generation of leaders, and will be honored. That is the ultimate mark a board chair wants to leave on an organization.

BOARD CHAIR'S TO DO LIST

✓ Put closure on tasks and relationships, and thank everyone for their contributions.

✓ Talk to others and think about ways to stay involved in the organization if so desired.

✓ Take an inventory of how the board chair experience has impacted your growth as a human being and as a leader.

✓ Decide how to use this experience in figuring out what's next for you.

✓ Reflect on the work you have accomplished for the good of the organization.

---

19. John Carver, *Boards that Make a Difference: A New Design for Leadership in Nonprofit and Public Organizations* (Hoboken, N.J.: John Wiley & Sons, 1997).

Appendix 1

Board Chair's To Do List: A Summary

PART I. THE FOUNDATION: *BUILDING INDIVIDUAL CAPACITY*

Saying Yes	The Board Chair's Role	Board Chair–Chief Executive Partnership	Communication and Facilitation Skills
✓ Talk to key organizational leaders and donors to learn more about specific board chair roles and responsibilities, the current work and future direction of the organization, and others' perceptions of the organization. ✓ Think about how saying yes to serve as chair may affect your relationships at home, at work, and at leisure. ✓ Take an inventory of personal strengths and limitations, and build on this self-awareness to maximize strengths and address limited skills and knowledge areas.	✓ Be a visionary leader. Empower the board to be innovative, creative, and take calculated risks. ✓ Develop and apply key leadership skills (including respect, humility, integrity, and communication) in accomplishing the key duties of the board chair role. ✓ Decide how you will balance routine tasks and those that surface unexpectedly. ✓ Uphold ethical and legal standards of conduct, and expect no less from every board member.	✓ Frame the partnership in the context of good governance practices. ✓ Be sensitive to the many variables that that can influence the success or failure of this key relationship, and have the courage to act to bring about change. ✓ Have clear mutual expectations around roles and responsibilities. ✓ Maintain open lines of communication. ✓ Periodically access the health of the partnership in areas of trust, respect, communication, purpose, expectations, attitudes, and boundaries.	✓ Focus on both the intent and delivery of the message being communicated. ✓ Apply communication skills differentially, taking into account the purpose of the exchange and the audience. ✓ Strengthen communication skills by listening, formulating proper questions, probing to achieve clarification and shared meaning, demonstrating empathy, confronting difficult issues or obstacles, and being attentive to content and group dynamics. ✓ Practice and ask for feedback from others on your use of effective communication and facilitation skills.

PART II. THE JOURNEY: *OPTIMIZING THE WORK OF THE BOARD*

Board Development	Generative Thinking and Decision Making	Board Work Structures
✓ Be proactive in using the board development model to identify and engage individuals as potential board members, maximize each board member's contributions to the board, and maintain engagement of outgoing board members. ✓ Ensure that board development initiatives exist for board member identification, orientation, sustainability, and preservation. ✓ Cultivate and sustain relationships with new, ongoing, or terminating board members for optimizing the work of the board. ✓ Manage individual and group issues that challenge the healthy functioning of the board.	✓ Be a generative thinker and ask catalytic questions. ✓ Facilitate robust dialogue at board meetings, and encourage big-picture thinking. ✓ Infuse generative thinking in board decisions and outcomes. ✓ Use the five-step decision-making model to support thoughtful and thorough board decisions and outcomes.	✓ Choose work structures that optimize the work of the board. ✓ Create meeting agendas that respect the available time and the purpose of the board. ✓ Use a consent agenda for disseminating information that does not require discussion or an immediate board vote. ✓ Keep the board informed and ensure fluid and appropriate communication. ✓ Address, don't ignore, obstacles limiting effective board communications.

Resource Development and Fiscal Oversight	Strategic and Program Planning	Performance Evaluation
✓ Be a role model and engage the board in resource development activities, which include providing financial support to the organization, attending fundraising events, identifying and cultivating donors, and making solicitations. ✓ In coordination with the chief executive and the development officer, be available as an asset in resource development activities. ✓ Help to educate and engage board members to ensure sound fiscal oversight of the organization.	✓ Ensure that the organization has a strategic plan. ✓ Oversee the hiring of a strategic planning consultant, if needed. ✓ Facilitate board communications around strategic planning. ✓ Maintain momentum in moving the strategic planning process forward, and match board engagement to the current strategic planning tasks. ✓ Encourage generative thinking in brainstorming new program ideas and initiatives. ✓ Work with the chief executive to create opportunities to educate the board about current programs and services. ✓ Apply program evaluation results to board decisions to expand, reduce, or eliminate existing programs and services.	✓ Ensure that the board conducts a board assessment, reviews the results, and implements change as needed. ✓ Conduct an annual performance evaluation of the chief executive and provide feedback supported by evidence and examples. ✓ Consider ways to obtain feedback about your performance as board chair. ✓ Decide what other evaluations to implement in support of the board's performance.

Part III. The Finale: *Creating Endings and New Beginnings*

Succession Planning	Reaching Closure, Looking Ahead, and Reflecting on the Experience
✓ Contribute to succession planning by identifying and assessing future leaders. ✓ Be available to mentor the incoming board chair and help with the leadership transition. ✓ Consider a range of options for mentoring an incoming board chair.	✓ Put closure on tasks and relationships, and thank everyone for their contributions. ✓ Talk to others and think about ways to stay involved in the organization if so desired. ✓ Take an inventory of how the board chair experience has impacted your growth as a human being and as a leader. ✓ Decide how to use this experience in figuring out what's next for you. ✓ Reflect on the work you have accomplished for the good of the organization.

Appendix 2

Using the Right Tools

Having the right tools can make the job of the board chair much easier. Two of these tools are sample letters and sample board meeting agendas. This appendix provides several useful samples; for ease of use, these samples are also available for download at www.boardsource.org/bch.

Sample Letters

A board chair may be required to write letters to board members and potential board members for a variety of reasons. In some cases, the letter may address a delicate situation such as asking a board member for a financial contribution or asking a board member to step off the board. In many instances the letters may be simply a confirmation to follow a face-to-face or telephone conversation. The letter should serve to help provide clarity to the board member and as an official documentation of the chair's action.

The sample letters in this section are designed to provide board chairs with some suggested language to use. *These letters are not intended to be used as is*, but should be customized to suit the needs of each board chair. The content can be incorporated into an e-mail as well. The sample letters included in this book provide examples for

- Asking a board member for an annual gift

- Asking a board member to step down

- Cultivating a prospective board member

- Recruiting a prospective board member

- Thanking an outgoing board member

SAMPLE LETTER: ASKING A BOARD MEMBER FOR AN ANNUAL GIFT

Dear Jim,

I am writing as follow-up to our phone conversation regarding the annual campaign.

It is my privilege and responsibility to seek financial support from all our board members to demonstrate our good faith in our organization. As we approach individuals and foundations for significant support, it is critical to demonstrate that we have 100 percent board participation. I am hopeful you will be able to maintain last year's level of giving and perhaps consider an increase.

We appreciate your valuable and active work for the organization. Your wise counsel makes a real difference.

Sincerely,

Ray Marcus
Board Chair

SAMPLE LETTER: ASKING A BOARD MEMBER TO STEP DOWN

Dear Alice,

This letter is not easy to write. You have been an important player in our foundation since its conception, and we are grateful for your energy and vision.

As we discussed during our meeting last week, the past year has been difficult for you since you began a new job that takes you out of town a lot. It has become increasingly apparent that other responsibilities make it difficult for you to be present for our board meetings.

You know how necessary it is for this organization to have the active interest and participation of each board member. Therefore, I hope you will understand my request that you resign before the end of your term so that we can appoint someone in your place.

We all hope that the day will come when your other activities will allow you to reconsider board membership in the future. We will miss you. As we discussed, the volunteer coordinator will be contacting you to explore other ways for you to stay involved. Thanks for all you have done on behalf of the organization.

Sincerely,

Patricia Williams
Board Chair

SAMPLE LETTER: CULTIVATING A PROSPECTIVE BOARD MEMBER

Dear Lucille:

I was delighted to get Jack's call to say that he had approached you about the possibility of serving on the board of directors of the Llama Protection Foundation (LPF). Under the leadership of a new chief executive, LPF is in the midst of implementing a new business plan. In addition to a strategic emphasis on community-level program activity, the plan calls for the reinvigoration of a board that has served us well but now needs fresh thinking, new ideas, and a more diverse set of experiences. I have attached a list of current board members for your perusal.

As Jack may have told you, each board member is elected to a three-year term, and can be reelected two times. Each member is expected to attend meetings and serve on at least one committee. At LPF, board members have ultimate responsibility not only for the financial well-being of the organization but also for working with staff in thinking strategically and planning for the efficient deployment of precious resources. Our board members are extremely busy people, so we try to best utilize their talent and knowledge without wasting time.

To that end, the board meets three times per year (a schedule is attached), starting over dinner on Monday evening and adjourning by 3:00 p.m. the following day. Each year, one meeting is lengthened by one day to provide for a retreat and/or tour of one of LPF's project areas.

Lucille, due in large measure to the wonderful support of your family, LPF is emerging as the premier llama protection organization in the nation. We have an enormous challenge before us if we are to achieve our mission. We need the kind of energy, commitment, and new ideas that you would bring to the board.

I will look forward to speaking with you in the near future, and of course would be more than pleased to meet you in New York or another convenient place. If for some reason you might be coming to Washington, D.C., I think you would enjoy meeting some of our senior staff and touring LPF's headquarters office. I will call in the next few days. In the meantime, please don't hesitate to call me if you have any questions about your role as a member of the board of directors.

Yours truly,

Jane Stewart
Board Chair

SAMPLE LETTER: RECRUITING A PROSPECTIVE BOARD MEMBER

Dear Jim,

I am writing you as the new chair of the Llama Protection Foundation (LPF). As you know, I have worked closely with George, your good friend, and he gave me your name as a potential board member.

My fellow board members and I believe that the Llama Protection Foundation needs to have a representative from the herding industry on our board. I would like for you to consider allowing me to forward your name to our governance committee. I can well imagine that you receive dozens of requests to join in the promotion of many worthy causes, but I believe that this organization might be especially of interest to you. Our purpose is to protect the dwindling gene pool of productive llamas and to promote practices that lead to a healthy population. We are currently operating with a $1.5 million budget and 15 employees across the country in four regional centers. Our headquarters are in Washington, D.C.; we have almost 10,000 members and capital financial assets of slightly more than $3 million.

Our board meets three times a year, and we try hard to focus our board members' talents on long-term strategic issues. The board is relatively small — 13 members — and we expect to increase it to 15 members before the end of the year. All of the board members are busy executive and professional people who insist that the organization be as creative and economical as possible in its demands on their energies and time. At board meetings, the members enjoy the serious, focused discussion on our goals, present and future, and on the deployment of our human and financial resources to assure our institutional success. I firmly believe you would find them and the very competent staff of imaginative and passionate individuals stimulating and exciting to work with.

I have enclosed a small packet of material, which will give you an idea of the work that LPF does. Please check our Web site at www.llamapf.org as well.

We are currently scheduled to talk by phone on Monday, January 31, at 9:45 a.m. I look forward to the conversation. Thank you for your consideration.

Regards,

Justin Matthews
Board Chair

SAMPLE NOTE: THANKING AN OUTGOING BOARD MEMBER

Dear Maria,

It was a pleasure serving with you on the Llama Protection Foundation board over the past two years. I appreciate your contributions as a dedicated board member. Your work as a member of the resource development committee helped us achieve our best annual campaign to date.

Thank you for your time and commitment to the board and LPF. I hope you will consider staying involved with LPF in new ways. Don't be a stranger!

With great appreciation,

Elizabeth Fuller
Board Chair

SAMPLES MEETING AGENDAS

The first sample agenda clarifies whether an agenda item is up for discussion or if a decision needs to be made. The second sample agenda is organized around board functions.

Sample Agenda 1

Llama Protection Foundation
123 Main Street
Washington, DC 20003

Meeting of the Board of Directors
October 20, 2007
7:00 p.m. – 9:00 p.m.

The mission of the Llama Protection Foundation is to protect the dwindling gene pool of productive llamas and to promote practices that lead to a healthy population.

A. General Business (5 minutes)

    a. Call to order and attendance

B. Approval of Consent Agenda (5 minutes)

    a. Approval of board meeting minutes

    b. Approval of meeting agenda

    c. Chief executive's report

    d. Committee reports

    e. Special events calendar

C. Discussions (60 minutes)

    a. New program started in January: update and next steps

    b. Next year's capital campaign

    c. Treasurer's report

D. Decision (45 minutes)

    a. Staff and program expansion proposal

E. Executive Session

    a. Reactions to today's board meeting

F Adjournment

Sample Agenda 2

Llama Protection Foundation
123 Main Street
Washington, DC 20003

Meeting of the Board of Directors
October 20, 2007
7:00 p.m. – 9:00 p.m.

The mission of the Llama Protection Foundation is to protect the dwindling gene pool of productive llamas and to promote practices that lead to a healthy population.

A. Call to order

B. Consent Agenda

    a. Approval of board meeting minutes

    b. Approval of meeting agenda

    c. Chief executive's report

    d. Committee reports

    e. Special events calendar

C. Program Planning and Evaluation

    a. Staff and program expansion proposal

    b. Update and next steps on new program

D. Finances and Resource Development

    a. Treasurer's Report

    b. Status of annual fundraising campaign

E. Adjournment

Suggested Resources

Axelrod, Nancy R. "Curious Boards." *Board Member*, May/June 2006.

Axelrod, Nancy R. *Culture of Inquiry: Healthy Debate in the Boardroom*. Washington, D.C.: BoardSource, 2007.

Bobowick, Marla J., Sandra R. Hughes, and Berit M. Lakey. *Transforming Board Structure: Strategies for Committees and Task Forces*. Washington, D.C.: BoardSource, 2001.

Chait, Richard P. *How To Help Your Board Govern More and Manage Less*. Washington, D.C.: BoardSource, 2002.

Chait, Richard P., William P. Ryan, and Barbara E. Taylor. *Governance as Leadership: Reframing the Work of Nonprofit Boards*. Hoboken, N.J.: John Wiley & Sons, 2005.

Connolly, Paul M. *Navigating the Organizational Lifecycle: A Capacity-Building Guide for Nonprofit Leaders*. Washington, D.C.: BoardSource, 2006.

Flynn, Outi. *Meet Smarter: A Guide to Better Nonprofit Board Meetings*. Washington, D.C.: BoardSource, 2004.

Gale, Robert. *Leadership Roles in Nonprofit Governance*. Washington, D.C.: BoardSource, 2003.

Lakey, Berit M. *The Board Building Cycle: Nine Steps to Finding, Recruiting, and Engaging Nonprofit Board Members*. 2nd ed. Washington, D.C.: BoardSource, 2007.

Kaner, Sam, Lenny Lind, Catherine Toldi, Sarah Fisk, and Duane Berger. *Facilitator's Guide to Participatory Decision-Making, Second Edition*. San Francisco, Calif.: Jossey-Bass, 2007.

Kissman, Katha. *Taming the Troublesome Board Member*. Washington, D.C.: BoardSource, 2006.

Kocsis, Deborah L. and Susan A. Waechter. *Driving Strategic Planning: A Nonprofit Executive's Guide*. Washington, D.C.: Board Source, 2003.

Kurtz, Daniel L. and Sarah E. Paul. *Managing Conflicts of Interest: Practical Guidelines for Nonprofit Boards*. 2nd ed. Washington, D.C.: BoardSource, 2006.

Lakey, Berit M. *Nonprofit Governance: Steering Your Organization with Authority and Accountability*. Washington, D.C.: BoardSource, 2000.

Lang, Andrew S. *Financial Responsibilities of Nonprofit Boards*. Washington, D.C.: BoardSource, 2003.

Lawrence, Barbara and Outi Flynn. *The Nonprofit Policy Sampler*. 2nd ed. Washington D.C.: BoardSource, 2006.

Light, Mark. *Executive Committee*. Washington, D.C.: BoardSource, 2004.

Mintz, Joshua and Jane Pierson. *Assessment of the Chief Executive*, revised ed. Washington, D.C.: BoardSource, 2005.

The Nonprofit Board Answer Book: A Practical Guide for Board Members and Chief Executives, 2nd ed. San Francisco and Washington, D.C.: Jossey-Bass and BoardSource, 2007.

Nonprofit Governance Index 2007. Washington, D.C.: BoardSource, 2007.

Ostrower, Francie and Marla J. Bobowick. "Nonprofit Governance and the Sarbanes-Oxley Act." Urban Institute National Survey of Nonprofit Governance: Preliminary Findings. 2006.

Patterson, Sally J. *Generating Buzz: Strategic Communications for Nonprofit Boards*. Washington, D.C.: BoardSource, 2006.

The Source: Twelve Principles of Governance That Power Exceptional Boards. Washington, D.C.: BoardSource, 2005.

Yankey, John A. and Amy McClellan. *The Nonprofit Board's Role in Planning and Evaluation*. Washington, D.C.: BoardSource, 2003.

About the Author

Mindy R. Wertheimer, Ph.D., LCSW, is the director of field education and faculty member of the School of Social Work, Georgia State University. In this role, she develops and conducts training that focuses on relationship building for human service professionals and students, serving more than 300 organizations in Atlanta and north Georgia. She is a certified *True Colors*® facilitator.

Dr. Wertheimer is a consultant and trainer for nonprofits, professional associations, local and state governments, foundations, and educational institutions. Her work encompasses board development and governance issues, leadership development, board restructuring, team building, goal setting, supervision, communications, strategic planning, and ethics. Dr. Wertheimer serves as a professional coach and mentor to new and ongoing board chairs. She also conducts training programs for new board chairs to strengthen their leadership skills in the context of strong governance practices. Dr. Wertheimer presents her work at national conferences.

Dr. Wertheimer is a past board chair of Jewish Family & Career Services in Atlanta. She was instrumental in facilitating board restructuring, board development, and strategic planning, and she initiated the creation of a community advisory group and a program planning and evaluation committee. When she completed her board chair term, the agency honored her with the creation of the Mindy R. Wertheimer, Ph.D., Program for Professional Enrichment and Education, which is dedicated to ongoing staff development.

Dr. Wertheimer can be contacted at mwertheimer@gsu.edu.